# THE
# TAXICAB

# THE TAXICAB

## An Urban Transportation Survivor

**GORMAN GILBERT & ROBERT E. SAMUELS**

The University of North Carolina Press
Chapel Hill & London

© 1982 The University of North Carolina Press
All rights reserved
Manufactured in the United States of America

Library of Congress Cataloging in Publication Data

Gilbert, Gorman, 1943–
The taxicab.

Bibliography: p.
Includes index.
1. Taxicabs—United States—History. I. Samuels,
Robert E., 1913– . II. Title.
HE5623.G53    388.4'1321    82-2726
ISBN 0-8078-1528-4    AACR2

To the memory of
Benjamin Samuels,
for nearly a half century
a leader, architect, and friend
of the taxicab industry

# CONTENTS

Acknowledgments
xiii

**CHAPTER 1**
Myths, Misconceptions, and Neglect
3

**CHAPTER 2**
European Ancestors of the Taxicab
8

**CHAPTER 3**
The Development of the Taxicab
25

**CHAPTER 4**
The Birth of Taxicab Fleets
38

**CHAPTER 5**
The Depression and Regulation
61

**CHAPTER 6**
War and Recovery
74

**CHAPTER 7**
Federal Involvement
86

**CHAPTER 8**
The Economics of Taxicab Operations
103

**CHAPTER 9**
Service Innovations
123

**CHAPTER 10**
Regulation and Deregulation
141

**CHAPTER 11**
Dimensions of Change
156

**CHAPTER 12**
The Survival of Private Enterprise in Public Transportation
170

Notes
181

Bibliography
187

Index
191

# TABLES AND FIGURES

**TABLES**

| | | |
|---|---|---|
| 3.1 | Urban Densities about 1898 | 27 |
| 3.2 | Early Automobile Production and Registration | 33 |
| 6.1 | War and Postwar Taxicab Trends | 77 |
| 6.2 | Distribution of Postwar Public Transportation Ridership | 84 |
| 6.3 | Taxicab Trip Length | 85 |
| 7.1 | Transit Operating Trends | 88 |
| 7.2 | Transit Service Trends | 89 |
| 7.3 | Public Ownership of Transit | 89 |
| 7.4 | Price of New York City Taxi Medallion | 92 |
| 8.1 | Taxicab Firms by Type | 106 |
| 8.2 | Distribution of Firm Sizes for United States | 107 |
| 8.3 | Taxi Supply Characteristics | 109 |
| 8.4 | Taxi Occupancy Rate | 112 |
| 8.5 | Characteristics of Taxi Users and Taxi Trips | 114 |
| 8.6 | Operating Costs | 119 |
| 8.7 | Operating Ratios Excluding Depreciation Costs | 120 |
| 8.8 | Revenue and Trip Length | 121 |
| 9.1 | Conventional Taxi Services | 126 |
| 9.2 | Characteristics of Twenty-eight General Market Taxi Systems (1979) | 129 |
| 9.3 | Summary of California Paratransit Operations (1976) | 130 |
| 9.4 | User-Side Subsidy Examples | 138 |

**FIGURE**

| | | |
|---|---|---|
| 9.1 | Taxi-Operated Paratransit Innovations | 127 |

# ILLUSTRATIONS

London cabriolet of 1823
20

A London "coffin cab"
21

A hansom cab in 1830s
23

Early electric hansom cab in New York City
36

Electric hansom cab in New York City getting a recharged battery installed
36

Typical taxicab in Chicago at the time of World War I
45

Central control tower of the first traffic light system, Michigan Avenue at Jackson Boulevard in Chicago
45

A taxicab of the 1920s with convertible rear roof
46

A Chicago Yellow Cab of the 1920s with the driver in his winter uniform
46

Chicago Yellow Cab driver trainees being taught the proper way to crank an engine
47

Benjamin Samuels, chairman of Chicago Yellow Cab, Inc.
60

A 1935 model taxi manufactured by Checker Motors Corporation
69

A Checker-built cab of the late 1930s
69

Morris Markin shown with a Checker cab in 1970
97

An experimental paratransit vehicle of the late 1970s
176

Interior of an experimental paratransit vehicle showing access for wheelchair passengers
176

An experimental paratransit vehicle of the late 1970s, this one built by Alfa-Romeo
177

# ACKNOWLEDGMENTS

This book is the result of shared efforts not only of the authors but also of the many persons who have contributed to the information contained herein. The taxicab industry is an extremely varied one composed of many highly individualistic operators. Without the willingness of these taxi operators to share their thoughts and experiences, this book would have suffered mightily.

The contributions of the early taxi owners, and those who knew them, have lent a particularly valuable historical perspective, which would have otherwise been unachievable. To name them all would be impossible, but we do wish to note particularly Ralph E. Oakland (now deceased), whose memories provided much of the background for the section on Checker Motors, Morris Markin, Frank Sawyer, John Pettit, whose association with W. Lansing Rothschild provided insight into the taxicab operations on the West Coast, Walter Jacobs, whose association with John Hertz provided us with information concerning the early days of the car rental industry, Marvin Glassman of Columbus, Ohio, Jerry Wilson of Fort Worth and many other cities, James P. Sinnott, who provided details of the Checker Motors operations in New York City, Pittsburgh, and Minneapolis, and many others. The International Taxicab Association has been equally generous in providing data and historical materials to document changes in the industry; Al LaGasse, executive vice-president of the association, deserves special thanks for his generosity in making these materials available to us.

Others have contributed by reviewing and commenting on drafts of this manuscript. Professor Edward Kaiser of the Department of City and Regional Planning at the University of North Carolina at Chapel Hill kindly and thoroughly reviewed a very early draft, as did Bill

Williams of Yellow Cab Company, Raleigh, North Carolina, and Richard V. Gallagher, publisher of *Taxicab Management*. Laurie Mesibov provided a critical perspective on the legal discussions in the book, as well as insightful suggestions that materially improved the clarity of the entire manuscript. Ann Zeltmann assisted ably in the bibliographical requirements of this book.

The preparation of this manuscript was greatly aided by the generosity of the University of North Carolina. The university provided a Kenan Leave which enabled one of the authors to devote substantial time to the manuscript. The Department of City and Regional Planning, particularly Dr. David Godschalk, chairman, was unhesitantly cooperative in making time available to pursue this project while minimizing the academic chores that so often interfere with the researching and writing of a book of this sort. And, of course, we are indebted to Judy Yates for her painstaking typing of this manuscript. Finally, we thank Hope Samuels and Carlean Gilbert, our wives, for the time and understanding that they gave to us throughout this endeavor.

To all these persons, we express our sincere gratitude.

# THE
# TAXICAB

# 1
## MYTHS, MISCONCEPTIONS, AND NEGLECT

Few industries in the United States are as poorly understood as is the taxicab industry. To many people taxicabs conjure up images of vices ranging from prostitution to illicit liquor; taxi drivers are viewed with suspicion; and driving a taxi is considered a job of last resort. The public knows little about how taxi firms are organized; for example, many persons think of Yellow Cab as a giant conglomerate that serves many cities.

These public images have one thing in common: they are all partially or entirely false. With few exceptions, taxi drivers are law-abiding citizens. Many have made their occupation a career, and a number have sent their children through college on their taxi earnings. A large percentage of taxi drivers are not employees but independent entrepreneurs who own or lease their vehicles. Taxis transport packages, supplies—such as blood—to hospitals, clients of human service agencies, elderly and handicapped persons, and children with special needs, and perform many other services requiring skilled and considerate care. And, of course, Yellow Cab is not a national corporation.

Yet the false images persist and are in large part responsible for many of the regulations imposed upon the taxi industry. Most cities require extensive data on would-be taxi drivers, including fingerprints, blood tests, and criminal record checks. In fact, taxi drivers—unlike bus drivers—are usually licensed by local police departments. Taxi operators are often restricted from transporting more than one party at one time, required to use taximeters to prevent them from cheating customers, and sometimes made to post signs in each vehicle warning passengers to note the name and number of the driver as a precaution in case of a criminal incident.

It is not difficult to understand the persistence of the public's view of the taxi industry. In earlier days the taxi driver was not always so virtuous and taxi services were a serious competitor for mass transit operations. Moreover, taxi operators have done little to promote a better image of themselves and to dispel the misconceptions.

There are other, more subtle reasons for the public's faulted view. The taxi industry lacks the technological attraction of rapid transit, light rail, and other more futuristic modes. Nor does it receive the publicity that large-scale bus systems get as a result of their visibility. Finally, it exists in the private, rather than the public sector. These reasons have no doubt made planners, public officials, and students of urban transportation content to ignore taxi ordinances while they focused on such programs as area rapid-transit systems, authorities, and developmental technologies.

Whatever the reasons, the result is clear: taxicabs have remained poorly understood and largely outside the funding programs that have bolstered public transportation, and local regulations concerning taxis have remained essentially unchanged and neglected and continue to be founded on an outmoded vision of the industry.

## THE INTEGRATED PARATRANSIT-TRANSIT DREAM

Despite the past—and present—neglect, the taxicab industry remains the key to a vision of a very different ordering of public transportation services. Rather than rely on the bus and rail systems currently serving larger United States cities, this new arrangement would employ a variety of flexible services which would supplement fixed-route services. In smaller cities such a program could provide the only public transportation services. These more flexible services are called *paratransit services*, meaning that they do not follow fixed routes.

The taxicab is the giant among paratransit providers. It can supply both exclusive-ride and shared-ride services. These terms refer to whether one passenger (or party) has exclusive use of a vehicle during a trip or whether the passenger (or party) shares the vehicle with

## Myths, Misconceptions, and Neglect / 5

other passengers whose trips begin or end at different places. The taxicab can be used in a subscription mode, a dial-a-ride mode, or a hailed-ride mode. These three options mean that service can be requested as a standing order—say, everyday at a specific time—by telephone a short time before a trip is desired, or by hailing a vehicle on the street. The taxi can provide demand-responsive neighborhood circulation services or feeder services to fixed-route transit. It can operate under contract to a public agency or under an arrangement by which users are subsidized directly by public agencies. In short, it can provide a wide range of paratransit services.

The vision of taxicab or paratransit services integrated with fixed-route transit is an exciting one. In many parts of our cities transit service is either nonexistent, poorly accessible, or inferior in overall quality or frequency. To persons in those areas the available transit services have too often fallen far short of meeting their travel needs. Yet, to expand or increase fixed-route transit service to these poorly served areas would be prohibitively expensive. For such areas paratransit services integrated with fixed-route services are an attractive option. For example, shared-ride taxi services can be provided in low-density neighborhoods to take persons to fixed-route transit terminals. Likewise, shared-ride taxis can provide mobility within neighborhoods.

Perhaps the most appealing aspect of integrated paratransit-transit services is that they provide the potential for an intangible yet critical factor: innovation. After decades of financial decline mass transit in the United States had become primarily publicly owned by the early 1970s. While much progress has been made in reversing the many effects of those decades of decline, much still needs to be accomplished if public transit is to provide the full range of services that the public requires. As a privately owned industry composed of locally owned enterprises, the taxi industry has the potential for injecting a much-needed infusion of imagination and entrepreneurial excitement into public transportation. A financially robust taxi industry properly included in the public transportation funding programs might provide the innovation and creativity that could lead to effective solutions to our transit problems.

# 6 / The Taxicab

## A VISION OF THE FUTURE—AND PAST

One of the most critical questions facing policymakers in urban transportation is why the vision of a healthy taxi industry fully integrated with fixed-route transit remains so far from reality. Part of the answer to this question has already been suggested. The taxi industry is no longer the financially healthy industry it was two or three decades ago, and the industry has done too little to change the public misconceptions about how it functions and what it does.

Too few people know how the industry evolved, why current regulations were enacted, what types of persons work in the industry, what range of services it provides, or that many taxi drivers are actually independent business persons. The scant media coverage that the industry receives is focused on rate increases and the cost of medallions in New York, the most atypical taxi city. The true picture of taxicab services in other cities has remained obscure, even for many transportation planners and policymakers.

The lack of public information about this very private industry is to be expected. While taxi firms could operate profitably without governmental subsidies or involvement in publicly funded programs, they had little reason to make information regarding costs, revenues, and productivity available to outsiders. The growth of public transit and human services programs in the 1970s dramatically changed this situation. Whereas taxi operators could once operate relatively free from public scrutiny, they must now participate in these publicly funded programs in order to survive, and public involvement means public information and data on operations. An industry which has always been rather circumspect, even internally, about divulging operating data, the taxi industry, increasingly, must report to public agencies.

This public-private tug-of-war is but one symptom of a larger dilemma facing both the industry and public policymakers. The entrepreneurial skills of taxi operators have enabled them to furnish services both more efficiently and at a lower cost than most public transit alternatives. Yet as taxi operators are incorporated into public programs, they must accept the same restrictions and constraints that now face public agencies, thereby negating the very advantages that the taxi industry can bring to the situation. The challenge facing local transportation decision makers is how to involve the private sector without destroying it.

Two premises underlie this book. The first is that taxi operators can and should be incorporated into public programs and that this involvement can be accomplished without destroying the advantages of the industry. The second is that this public policy dilemma can be resolved only by first raising substantially the general level of understanding about the taxi industry.

This book addresses the need for a better understanding of the industry by tracing the history of taxi services. This history has never before been written; nor is it an easy history to write. Accurate data on taxi operations are scarce, and the industry developed in tandem with the transit industry. To allow for the latter problem the following chapters also trace the development of transit services and provide a necessary background against which to understand how and why the taxi industry evolved. The lack of accurate data, however, is not so easily remedied. Records from within and without the industry have been examined. Several taxi operators have freely shared their early records and historical information. Some of the early pioneers of the industry have also shared their personal reflections of how the industry began.

Treating current conditions and trends within the industry, as well as major public policy issues such as deregulation, the book also focuses on the contemporary taxi industry and how it can be brought into the realm of public policy without destroying it.

It has been said that anyone who ever closely examines an industry concludes that the industry is in transition. Certainly this assessment is true for the taxi industry. More important, however, it is equally true of urban transportation in general. Limited petroleum supplies; mobility needs of the handicapped, the poor, and the aged; enormous transit deficits—these are but a few of the problems facing urban transportation. The taxi industry offers the potential for alleviating these problems, and that is, after all, the most important reason for studying the taxicab industry.

# 2

# EUROPEAN ANCESTORS OF THE TAXICAB

## THE BEGINNING OF PUBLIC TRANSPORTATION

The development of urban transportation can be traced back to the very earliest human settlements. For many centuries cities were strategically located along the waterways, and boatmen plied these waterways carrying both goods and people. In Egypt, for instance, relics dating back to about 4000 B.C. show clear evidence of boats carrying persons along the Nile. One example, in the Egyptian Museum in Cairo, is a model from approximately 2000 B.C. of a wooden boat used to carry a boatman and one passenger. Much later, in the cities of medieval Europe, boats were still the predominant form of urban transportation. In London these boats were called "wherries," a name still in use in the nineteenth century.[1] Even on the mythical River Styx a boatman named Charon transported the dead, thereby attaining the dubious distinction of being the first franchised boatman.

In the seventeenth century, however, urban transport underwent a major change. For the first time transportation in urban areas became truly "public." This is not to say that there had never been local transportation or that cities had not existed before 1600; cities had long flourished throughout the world, and their citizens had been carried by various means for centuries. However, it was the rich and the noble who enjoyed these transport services, not the public in general. Transportation for ordinary urbanites began to evolve only after the technological advances and rapid urbanization of the 1600s. Yet even in the seventeenth century public transportation was not yet affordable for the poor, who had to wait until the nineteenth century for public transportation to become inexpensive enough to serve them.

There is a simple reason why land-based urban transport had not evolved prior to the 1600s. Although cities had existed since about 3000 B.C., they had remained small in geographic size until late in the Middle Ages. For example, the ancient city of Ur is variously estimated to have had a population of 24,000 to 34,000 people in 2000 B.C. at a density of 120 to 200 people per acre.[2] Most ancient cities, however, were far smaller than Ur; the average city probably contained no more than 5,000 people.

After centuries of development the cities of medieval Europe were still quite small. In his history of urban development in Europe, Gutkind reports that Paris—one of the largest cities of the Middle Ages—had a population of only 60,000 in 1292 and 90,000 in 1350.[3] He also estimates that London's population totaled only 17,850 in 1086 and about 35,000 in 1377. Paris had an estimated density of 64 persons per acre in 1292, meaning that it covered an area of only about one and one-half square miles.[4] For the small, compact medieval cities, destinations were close, and walking was the primary mode of urban transportation. In fact, not until the eleventh century did the horse collar become widely used, significantly improving the efficiency of land transport.[5]

By the end of the sixteenth century the development of commerce was changing the lives of urban dwellers, as cities grew along harbors and rivers. The coming of the Renaissance and the Reformation brought new industries, such as herring fishing and the production of iron and cloth. Cultural exchange increased markedly with the increase in long-distance travel. Into the towns and cities came craftsmen, artists, and philosophers. Cities grew as centers of culture, government, commerce, and industry. This urbanization increased the size of cities and brought with it the need for better intraurban transportation. The dramatic urbanization of the sixteenth and seventeenth centuries transformed the larger cities from "walking" cities to "vehicle" cities.

The growth of London and Paris illustrates the scope of urbanization during the sixteenth and seventeenth centuries. London grew from 75,000 in 1500 to 200,000 in 1600, 450,000 in 1660, and 675,000 in 1700.[6] One century later London had 864,000 residents. Paris had

100,000 residents in the middle of the sixteenth century and had grown scarcely at all over the previous two hundred years. The end of the sixteenth century, however, brought the beginning of the construction of fine houses, gardens, bridges, and the first efforts to construct streets in straight lines. With the onset of the seventeenth century Paris grew rapidly and began to absorb its suburbs. By 1801 Paris had 550,000 people.[7]

After centuries of extremely slow growth, London, Paris, and other European cities had grown enormously in a period of 150 years. An obvious consequence—and perhaps cause—of this growth was that the larger European cities were too large for residents to rely on walking as their only way of getting around. A new, faster means of urban transportation was necessary.

Soon after 1600, first in Paris and shortly thereafter in London, the horse-drawn hackney appeared, usually standing outside inns waiting to be hired. As early as 1623 in London the wherry operators were protesting that the hackneys "rob us of our livings and carry 500 fares from us."[8] Their protests proved fruitless, however; hackneys were to dominate urban transport for more than two hundred years.

The word *hackney* was derived from the ancient French word *haquenée*, meaning an ambling horse or mare, usually ridden by ladies, or a horse of middling size and quality used for riding, but not for war or hunting. Chaucer used the word in that connotation in the fourteenth century.[9] From an early date the word was also used to indicate a horse available for hire and was later expanded to include a carriage for hire, in that case from a livery stable. (The leasing of vehicles for public transportation had its origin at a very early time. The term *livery* is still used today to mean certain vehicles available for hire.) One can surmise the prevailing attitude toward this early form of public transportation by the entry in Samuel Pepys's *Diary* for 18 April 1664: "Myself being in a hackney and full of people, was ashamed to be seen by the world, many of them knowing me."

The hackney is the earliest direct ancestor of both the taxicab and mass transit. These vehicles were available for hire and followed no fixed routes or schedules. In 1634 in London a retired mariner named Baily had four fine hackney coaches built and stationed them not in front of inns but rather in the Strand, next to St. Mary's Church, thereby creating the first example of what later became known as a "stand," but which in those days was called a "standing." Baily's hackney stand became so popular with hackney drivers that crowding soon forced drivers to drive along the streets looking for and soliciting passengers. Known then as "plying for hire," this practice is today called "cruising." In Paris in 1648 the innkeeper at the Sign of St. Fiacre had the idea of keeping carriages for hire at his inn. This became one of the first hackney stands in Paris, and within a short time the vehicles themselves were called "fiacres," a name still in use today. The hackney stand was called a "place de fiacre," and a coachman was called a "cocher de fiacre."

Hackney drivers were seldom the owners of the their vehicles; drivers usually paid a daily fee to rent a horse and coach, a system which in the twentieth century was rediscovered and called "leasing." One of the earliest lessors of coaches and horses was Tobias Hobson of Cambridge, who always placed the horse that he wanted the driver to take in the first stall. An otherwise undistinguished man, Hobson lives on in the expression "Hobson's choice."

These early seventeenth-century public hackney stands were the forerunners of many to be established in the next three centuries. They were popular because they diverted hackneys from plying for hire (where they contributed to traffic congestion) and placed them at accessible places known to the public. The hackney stands were generally in the public ways, but the notion of private hackney stands in the middle of inn yards for the convenience of the patrons spread to include private hackney stands on the streets at hotels, private hackney stands on lots owned by the hackney operators, and private arrangements with railroad stations and other locations. The inducement for these private arrangements was the fact that a sufficient number of vehicles would be available to serve customers of the establishments. This practice of private stands persisted in the United States until the middle of the twentieth century.

Charles I was most displeased by the traffic congestion that resulted from the popularity of the hackney coaches. In 1634, in an attempt to reduce their numbers by competition, he gave Sir Saunders Duncomb the exclusive right to rent out sedan chairs. Sedan chairs were in use on the Continent in large numbers and were very popular among the well-to-do but, at the time, were not known in England. Because the chairs were carried on the bearers' shoulders, which connoted slave labor, they were not very popular in London until nearly a hundred years later when a new version was built which permitted the chairs to be carried at arms' length with the bearers' arms extending straight downward. Duncomb's few chairs did little to alleviate the traffic congestion; the number of hackney coaches in London grew.

While neither a sleek nor a comfortable vehicle, the hackney possessed the one essential for survival: it was sturdy. Even in the large cities streets were a challenge, both for vehicles and pedestrians. Only the principal thoroughfares were paved, usually with cobblestones. There were no sidewalks, and the narrowness of the streets made walking treacherous. Garbage was thrown into the streets, and street lighting, which consisted of candles in a window of every tenth house, did little to discourage muggers. In this environment the durability of the hackney was essential. At the same time, the hackney carriages, along with the ever-heavier private carriages, were doing their share of damage to the unpaved streets. As one anonymous wit proclaimed: "The streets, some time ago, were paved with stones, which, aided by a hackneycoach, half broke your bones."

The life of a hackney driver had rewards. Hackneys were often coaches previously used by noble families and were sometimes still adorned by the trappings of their former owners. Drivers employed men known as "watermen" or "caddies" to water and look after their horses while the drivers awaited passengers by drinking in taverns or sleeping atop their vehicles. The caddies also opened the doors for passengers. Yet those amenities were doubtless far less important than the image that hackney drivers enjoyed among the females of the eighteenth century. Moore reports that "no self-respecting member of the profession was ever without at least one lady-love" and girls "considered it the summit of happiness to be seen leaning on the arm of a hackney-coachman."[10]

Like other public transportation modes, the hackney was not to last forever. By the early 1800s the hackney industry had fallen into disfavor. The filthy condition of the carriages, together with the hostile and dishonest drivers who drove them in a reckless manner, provoked much public outcry for regulation of the hackney trade. A writer to the *London Magazine* in 1825, signing only the name "Jehu," complained at length about the condition of the carriages and the dishonesty of the drivers and suggested that many arguments over the amount of the fare could be avoided if there were "a pedometer visible to the unfortunate freight to be noted upon entering, to be noted on exiting. . . . It would save endless altercations, it would save typographying a table of hackney-coach fares, it would save a man's money and temper, and go far towards saving the souls of hackney-coachmen born, or to be born—the troubles of the commissioners."[11]

Jehu's idea was not a new one. Historians recount that in Roman times a runner with a sack of small stones went along with a hired chariot. Discarding one stone every so many paces, he provided an accurate record of the distances traveled. The Romans also used a candle with markings on the side to measure the time spent on long chariot trips, thereby computing the cost of the trip. In China a vehicle called "giligulicha" (a "counting mile drum car") was in use in the Ch'in Dynasty, about 200 B.C. Pictures of the giligulicha show a two-story, single-axle cart pulled by three horses and seating perhaps twelve passengers. On the lower story a wooden figure of a man carried a drum, which struck every li; on the upper story a second wooden figure held a gong, which struck every ten li. A li was supposed to represent the distance covered in one-tenth of an hour's march and was variously said to be 479 yards and 699 yards.

Despite Jehu's suggestion and the earlier uses of distance meters, the hackney owners did not experiment with metering devices. Nor did the majority of the hackney owners keep their vehicles clean or hire respectable drivers. By 1841 there were only four hundred hackneys in London, and by 1851 they were almost nonexistent.

In retrospect, the demise of the hackney was inevitable. While "public" in the sense that it was available to anyone with enough to pay the fare, the hackney was too expensive for most people. Moore reports that hackney fares in the early 1800s were one shilling for the first mile and sixpence for each additional half-mile. At that time in New York City the hackney fares were twenty-five cents to thirty-seven and a half cents for the first mile. In both cases the fares were prohibitively expensive for working-class individuals, who still had no choice but to walk. As newer, faster, and cheaper modes, such as the cabriolet, were developed, the hackney vanished.

Yet the hackney is extremely important in the history of public urban transport. It was the first public transportation used by the general public, and it lasted over two centuries. Thus, it was the first mode which challenged public officials with problems of congestion, service quality, and fare levels and became the subject of the first regulation of urban public transportation. This regulatory structure has continued to influence how public bodies attempt to regulate public transportation. Although the hackney succumbed to its more modern competitors, it left a lasting mark on urban transportation.

## THE HACKNEY AND PUBLIC POLICY

Regulation of various industries had been established in England long before the hackney. In fact, the United States Supreme Court many centuries later noted: "It has been customary in England from time immemorial and in this country from its first colonization, to regulate ferries, common carriers, hackmen, bakers, millers, warfingers, innkeepers, etc."[12] "Time immemorial" is said to be that time "when the memory of man runneth not to the contrary," a time later fixed by Parliament to be 1189 when Richard I became king. While the hackney was not the first industry to be regulated in England, it was the first example of urban transportation regulation. At least the regulations enacted to control hackneys were more extensive than those which had previously existed.

The very success of the hackney made it the subject of regulations. In the first half of the seventeenth century the number of hackneys had grown so large that traffic congestion had become a problem for the nobility, whose carriages the hackney traffic impeded. Concerned about his passage along the streets of London, Charles I ordered in 1635 that hackneys be licensed, although the lack of police made the enforcement of his edict difficult, if not impossible. His proclamation of 19 January 1635 barred the use of hackney carriages in London and Westminster except for trips going outside of those areas for a distance of at least three miles. His proclamation "to restrain the multitude and promiscuous use of coaches" stated that "hackney coaches were a great disturbance to his Majesty, his dearest consort the Queen, the nobility and others of place and degree in their passage through the streets."[13] He went on to state that the hackney coaches broke up the pavements of the streets and drove up the prices of hay and provender.

The 1635 law was not effective in controlling the hackneys and the congestion that they caused. In 1654 Parliament placed a limit of three hundred on the number of hackneys in London and Westminster and required each hackney licensee to have two horses per hackney. This law also placed the regulation of hackneys in the hands of the London Court of Aldermen. During the year of his coronation, 1660, Charles II issued a proclamation forbidding hackneys from plying for hire on the streets. It is doubtful, however, whether this proclamation had much effect. Samuel Pepys commented in his diary, "Notwithstanding that this was the first day of the king's proclamation against hackney coaches coming into the streets to stand to be hired, yet I got one to carry me home."[14]

The hackney had created a public policy dilemma. If hackneys were unrestricted, they would create traffic problems. Regulations to limit the number of hackneys, however, would create problems of enforcement and of fair allocation of licenses among would-be hackney operators. That dilemma continues to be relevant over three centuries later.

The English approach to these problems was continued regulation. In 1660 Parliament imposed a tax of twenty shillings per hackney to pay for the regulation of hackneys and a license fee of five pounds to pay for the damage to the streets that they caused. The following year, Charles II appointed commissioners whose duties included the regulation and licensing of hackney coaches. The number of carriages was raised from three hundred to four hundred. Regulations limited who could have licenses (for example, no licensee could have another trade) and put other restrictions on coaches and horses. In 1694 Parliament raised the number of hackney licenses to seven hundred.

Throughout the eighteenth century hackneys flourished in London, and the pressure for additional hackney licenses continued.

However, no one was allowed a hackney license unless he was recommended by a member of Parliament, which meant that members, their friends, and their former servants dominated the industry. These hackney owners realized that their economic self-interest was served by restricting the number of licenses. In 1768, the number of licenses was increased to one thousand, but it was never to exceed that figure.

During these years other types of hackney regulations were also enacted. The year of the plague, 1665, saw the enactment of an ordinance in London requiring hackney coaches to be aired for five days after carrying passengers to the pest houses. In 1695 the first commissioner for licensing hackney coaches was appointed. Seventy-three years later, George III created a commission to regulate hackney coaches. It approved the locations of standings throughout London and licensed caddies at those standings to water the horses, to take care of the hackneys in the absence of the drivers, and to assist passengers. The act creating the commission also required coachmen to give way to "persons of quality and gentlemen's coaches" (at a penalty of five pounds).

Comprehensive regulation of personal public transportation by acts of Parliament, proclamations, by-laws, and regulations, began with the London Hackney Carriage Act of 1831. That act, together with the London Hackney Carriages Act of 1843, is the basis for all modern regulation of demand-responsive vehicles. The 1831 act regulated drivers and their licensing, regulated hours and days of work, and forbade refusing passengers, abusive language, furious driving, drunken driving, blocking traffic, and overcharging passengers. It also provided for the return of lost property, required a license in the form of a metal plate affixed to the hackney vehicle, provided for standings, and defined standing for hire and plying for hire. Finally, it forbade taking additional passengers without the consent of the first passenger.

The act of 1843 broadened public regulation of hackneys still further. First, it provided for the inspection of coaches and horses. More important, it resolved a legal issue which had been a matter of interest for decades. It declared that the relationship between a driver and a hackney owner was that of servant and master with respect to responsibility for damages caused by the driver's neglect, regardless of whether or not the driver leased the coach. Thus, a party incurring damages could recover from the owner as well as the driver. The act also provided, however, for drivers to pay compensation for damage they caused to property. The regulation of drivers had begun earlier under the act of 1838, which was repealed and incorporated into the act of 1843. From the first, drivers were licensed by the police.

These early English laws show that public transportation has been a matter of public policy concern for three hundred years. The hackney, and not the taxicab in the twentieth century, first raised the issues of supply limitations, fare structures, driver licensing, vehicle standards, stands, and competition. Given the importance of English law in the development of law in the United States, it is not surprising that the regulatory approaches taken by the English to control hackneys were borrowed much later by United States cities to control taxicabs.

## THE EMERGENCE OF FIXED-ROUTE TRANSIT

It was inevitable that someone would decide to operate hackneys over designated routes at predetermined times. In 1661, French mathematician Blaise Pascal petitioned the Parisian government for permission to operate hackneys over five routes on a regular schedule.[15] In January of the following year permission was granted and the service began. It was, however, short-lived: the government forbade workmen, laborers, and soldiers from using these fixed-route hackneys, and the service had ceased by 1675.[16] Not until a century and a half later did fixed-route transit make a successful appearance. With the introduction of the omnibus in Paris in 1823, fixed-route transit began an evolution which was to separate it from the demand-responsive services, the taxicab and its predecessors.

Not unlike many inventions, the omnibus was an accidental development. Dunbar reports that Stanislas Baudry began operating scheduled, fixed-route vehicles from central Paris to some public baths that he owned in the suburb of Nantes. The downtown terminus was in front of a store owned by M. Omnes, who had coined the promotional slogan for his store: "Omnes for all." When Baudry found that people were using the vehicles but not his baths, he became a transportation entrepreneur and called his vehicles "omnibuses." By 1828 he had twelve omnibus routes in Paris.

The omnibus soon spread to other cities and countries. George Shillibeer, a onetime coach builder in Paris, left France to begin an omnibus service in his native London. His omnibus, called the Shillibeer, was pulled by three horses and began operation in July 1829. This heavy and cumbersome vehicle was later replaced by a lighter vehicle pulled by two horses and accommodating twelve to fifteen passengers.[17]

The success of the omnibus was not entirely beneficial for the operators. Unregulated competition increased to the point that in 1831 London omnibus operators formed an association to oversee their own operations. This association removed from service thirty-three of the ninety omnibuses then in existence.[18] Later, in 1857, the London General Omnibus Company bought out most of the omnibus operators and unified the omnibus operation.[19] Shillibeer, the man who brought the omnibus to London, eventually left the industry to become an undertaker.

The omnibus was not long in reaching the New World. Taylor reports that as early as 1830 at least 70 omnibus coaches were operating in New York City. However, the number was soon to increase to 255 in 1846 and to peak at 683 in 1853.[20]

Unlike the hackney, the omnibus was able to provide mobility to persons of modest economic means. Omnibus fares even declined during the 1830–60 era in the United States. Taylor reports that the typical omnibus fare in the 1830s was twelve and a half cents; by 1860 the typical fare had fallen to four to six cents. This fare was not affordable for everyone, but it did mean that a much larger segment of the population could take advantage of public transportation.

In 1855 in Paris an omnibus was placed on rails, thus creating the first urban street railway in Europe. This new service, the horsecar, had actually been invented in New York City in 1832. In 1859 the horsecar appeared in England, where it was called a "tram," a name derived from the wooden rails (trams) on which it ran.[21] Successive improvements to the horsecar enlarged its size and replaced the horses with electric traction.

## THE EVOLUTION OF THE TAXICAB

While fixed-route transit was evolving from the omnibus to the horsecar to the streetcar, the non-fixed-route services were also evolving into what eventually became the taxicab. In recent years the term *paratransit* has been used to label these services, and it can be applied retrospectively to a variety of services, including the hackney and its many successors.

One important successor appeared in Paris about 1800. The "cabriolet" was a fast, light, two-wheeled chaise drawn by one horse. It had a hood of wood or leather and an ample apron to cover the lap and legs of the occupant. (A letter to the *Public Advertiser* in 1798, written from France, described a person who had been "crushed to death by one of those machines called cabriolets; on account of which infernal vehicles, the inhabitants can no longer venture on foot at any hour.") At first, these vehicles had only two seats and accommodated only one passenger. Later the driver was moved to an outrigger seat, thereby increasing the capacity to two passengers. The cabriolets were fast, very uncomfortable, and dangerous.

Just after 1800 cabriolets appeared in London, where the name was quickly shortened to "cab," a name which was initially considered vulgar.[22] Cabs were popular, but the regulations granting hackney owners exclusive rights to transport Londoners hindered the spread of the cabs. Hackney owners initially opposed the cabs and predicted that they would not last. In 1805 nine cabs were licensed to two members of Parliament, and the hackney operators, observing the popularity of these new faster vehicles, quickly petitioned to have their licenses transferred to cabs. However, the early cab operators were men of high social standing who used their power to restrict the issuance of cab licenses to hackney operators. Not until 1832 did the hackney owners receive permission to transfer their licenses to cabs. Soon there were several hundred cabs on London streets.[23]

20 / The Taxicab

*London cabriolet of 1823. Driver's seat is on the side of the vehicle; two seats for passengers are located behind the drawn curtain. (From Henry Charles Moore,* Omnibuses and Cabs.*)*

At the same time the life-styles of urban populations were changing radically. The new middle class, with money and position, emulated the rich. Their clothing was expensive, and they were concerned with cleanliness. As a result they were very displeased with the dirty hackney coaches.[24] This group took to the cabriolets, and a major change in public passenger transportation had begun.

The intensity of the public rejection of the hackney carriage can be surmised from the popular publications of the day. Charles Dickens, one of the most incisive social critics of the time, devoted an entire chapter in *Sketches by Boz* to "Hackney-Coach Stands." He opened his commentary by describing the Edinburgh, Liverpool, and Manchester hackney stands:

*A variation of the cabriolet called the "coffin cab" in London in 1820s. (From Henry Charles Moore,* Omnibuses and Cabs.*)*

We readily concede to these places the possession of certain vehicles, which may look almost as dirty, and even go almost as slowly, as London hackney-coaches; but that they have the slightest claim to compete with the metropolis, either in point of standards, drivers, or cattle, we indignantly deny.... Why should hackney-coaches be clean? Our ancestors found them dirty and left them so. Why should we, with feverish wish to "keep moving," desire to roll along at the rate of six miles per hour, while they were content to rumble over the stones at four?... Or why should people be allowed to ride quickly at eightpence a mile, after Parliament had come to the solemn decision that they should pay a shilling a mile for riding slowly?[25]

In 1834, Joseph Hansom, an English architect, patented a new, low-slung vehicle. It had two huge (seven-foot, six-inch diameter) wheels, a front seat for the driver, and space for two passengers inside. A second version required the passengers to board the vehicle *through* the wheels![26] In 1836 Hansom's patent was sold, and among the purchasers was John Chapman, a London cab operator. Chapman made many improvements, such as moving the driver to the rear to give better balance and constructing a trap door in the roof through which directions could be given to the driver. From that time to the end of the century many different versions of this new vehicle were designed and put into service, but all carried the sobriquet "hansom cab."

Hansom's patents and the improvements patented by Chapman were incorporated into a company called the Hansom Patent Safety Cab. The company fiercely litigated against a horde of imitators, but ultimately collected very little in monetary damages. The company's many Jewish employees called these interlopers "shofuls," a Yiddish word for "worthless stuff" or "rubbish," and the expression was soon taken up by the public (variously spelled "showfull," "shouful," "schoefell," "shofle," "schoful").[27] Generally, the slang English word meant "counterfeit" and was widely used as such, but by mid-century it had been applied to hansom cabs so often that the inference of "counterfeit" had wholly disappeared, and all hansom cabs were called "showfulls" or "shofuls."[28]

*A hansom cab in 1830s. The original hansom design had solid wheels with a cut-out through which passengers entered the side of the vehicle. This later version has the passenger door at the rear of the vehicle. (From Henry Charles Moore,* Omnibuses and Cabs.*)*

Other less popular vehicles were also developed. An enclosed, four-wheeled cab was developed in 1823 and became known as a "clarence" (after the Duke of Clarence—later King William IV) or later as a "growler." About 1832 a small box-like cab accommodating two passengers seated face-to-face appeared. This vehicle was called a "back door cab" or a "minibus." At about the same time, the "victoria" appeared, named, of course, after the queen who was crowned in 1837.[29] It was a light, low, four-wheeled carriage having a collapsible hood, with seats (usually) for two persons and an elevated seat in front for the driver.[30] It proved to be very popular, particularly with the ladies, who could be seen while riding in it.

Thus the development of paratransit vehicles continued. By this time paratransit and mass transit were on very different paths, but both would continue to be influenced by the same technological developments. At the end of the nineteenth century the steam engine, the Otto cycle internal combustion engine, and electric traction were about to revolutionize both the transit and paratransit industries. The taxicab and the streetcar were about to be born.

# 3

# THE DEVELOPMENT OF THE TAXICAB

The taxicab industry in the United States emerged near the beginning of the twentieth century. As they had in Europe, the hackney, the cabriolet, the hansom cab, and other horse-drawn vehicles had served American cities in the 1800s. However, the first vehicle to be called a "taxicab" did not appear until after the turn of the century. Not unlike most new phenomena, the development of the taxicab did not occur as an isolated event; it was strongly influenced by the continuing evolution of mass transit vehicles and by the massive changes that were occurring in urban life.

## GROWTH AND CHANGE IN URBAN LIFE

The three decades spanning the turn of the century were marked by dramatic changes in technology, demographic patterns, and life-styles. They were also decades of inventions, urbanization, migration, and eventually a major war. Finally, they were the decades that gave birth to the automobile, the streetcar, the bus, and the taxicab.

Nowhere were these changes more evident than in urban areas. The entire United States was growing rapidly; the population increased from 50.6 million in 1885 to 100.5 million in 1915. It was, however, in urban areas where this growth was focused. In 1880 the country had only eight cities of 250,000 or more population. Forty years later it had twenty-five such cities. The nation, which had been only 28.8 percent urban in 1880, was predominantly (51.2 percent) urban in 1920.

Much of this growth was attributable to the heavy stream of immigrants arriving primarily from Europe. During the thirty years considered here over 19 million migrants came to the United States. The majority of these new residents came soon after 1900; between 1905 and 1910 nearly 5 million immigrants came, the most for any five-year period in United States history.[1] They settled primarily in the booming industrial cities of the Northeast; as early as 1890 four out of five persons living in greater New York were foreign born or had parents who were foreign born.[2] During the first decade of the twentieth century, American cities added 11,826,000 new residents. Of those, 41 percent were foreign immigrants and 29.8 percent were migrants from rural America.[3]

One immediate effect of the immigrant flood was crowding. Cities had always been fairly densely settled. Parts of Paris in 1329 and London in 1695 are estimated to have had about 222 persons per acre.[4] Portions of those cities reached maximum densities of about 312 persons per acre in the industrial era of the middle and late nineteenth century.[5] The same industrialization also increased densities in United States cities. There the overall urban densities were lower than in Europe, as can be seen in the estimates made by Weber in his classic 1898 study (see Table 3.1).[6]

Weber also computed a density of 15.2 persons per acre for twenty-eight American cities and 38.3 for twenty-two cities in Great Britain. However, those figures mask the tremendous variations within cities. Clark estimates that New York in 1900 had areas with 547 persons per acre.[7] Glaab and Brown report for the Tenth Ward in New York in 1898 a density of 757 persons per acre, a density which they suggest may have been the highest in the world.[8] They also estimate that the portion of New York City below the Harlem River had a density of about 143 persons per acre in the 1890s. That figure is higher than their estimates for Paris (126.9) and Berlin (100.8).[9] For seven of the ten largest cities, Glaab and Brown estimate that one of every four wards had densities exceeding 100 persons per acre.[10]

No doubt one factor influencing urban growth was the relatively stable and prosperous economic climate of the United States. With the exception of the recession of 1893–94, these three decades were generally years of economic health. Consumer prices were stable or declining from 1885 to 1900, after which they rose slowly until 1910.

In fact, measured in constant dollars, consumer prices were lower in 1900 than they had been in 1885. Real personal income was also relatively stable, but generally increasing during this time period, with the exception of the decreases in 1893 and 1894. Despite the influx of new foreign workers, unemployment rates remained reasonably low, as the industrializing economy absorbed large numbers of untrained workers.

Cities were busy places during the years between 1885 and 1915. They were growing rapidly and accepting tremendous numbers of new residents from the farms and from abroad. They were building factories to make the products of an age of invention and discovery. They were also crowded. Together, these developments made cities during these three decades a conducive environment for the incubation and growth of modern public transportation.

TABLE 3.1. *Urban Densities about 1898*

| City | Population per Acre |
|---|---|
| London | 75.5 |
| Paris | 65.8 |
| Berlin | 68.8 |
| New York | 13.0 |
| Chicago | 10.7 |
| Baltimore | 23.0 |
| Philadelphia | 12.6 |
| Brooklyn | 44.6 |
| Kansas City | 6.4 |
| St. Louis | 11.5 |
| Boston | 18.5 |

Source: Weber, *Growth of Cities*, p. 468.

## MASS TRANSIT: THE AGE OF THE STREETCAR

By the latter half of the nineteenth century the horsecar had firmly established itself as the dominant form of mass transit. Developed in 1832 in New York by John Stephenson, the horsecar did not become common until the late 1840s when rails were laid flush with the street surface.[11] One factor which encouraged the development of the horsecar was the prohibition of steam railroad operations in several cities, such as New York and Philadelphia, in the mid-1800s.[12] Passenger trains entering those cities were forced to stop and replace the locomotive with a team of horses. Although this was a cumbersome procedure, it demonstrated the increased efficiency that resulted from mounting horse-drawn vehicles on rails.

Usually, horsecars were pulled by two horses, although a few were pulled by four horses. The speed of a horsecar is reported by Smerk to have been about four miles per hour.[13] However, Taylor estimates the speed at six to eight miles per hour. Regardless, its speed was considerably higher than that of the omnibus, which it replaced. Its main advantage, however, was its higher capacity. A two-horse horsecar could seat forty passengers and accommodate over thirty standees, a capacity two to four times as great as that of the omnibus. It is not surprising that the horsecar was viewed by one contemporary as "the improvement of the age."[14]

Soon the horsecar was supplanting the omnibus as the primary mass transit mode. By 1860 horsecars were operating in the major cities; in Philadelphia alone eighteen firms were operating 155 miles of horsecar lines. By 1880 nearly every United States city of over fifty thousand in population had horsecars; about nineteen thousand horsecars ran on over three thousand miles of track.[15] Although the five-cent fare was a considerable sum for persons who earned only slightly more than a dollar a day, the use of the horsecar spread.

In the inventive times of the late nineteenth century, the idea of replacing the horse as a means of locomotion was the inspiration for much effort and innovation. The care and feeding of horses and the manure that they produced were both major problems. In addition, horses had difficulty in hilly terrain; in some instances the horses were placed aboard the horsecars to ride downhill and then reattached to the front of the horsecar at the bottom of the hill.

Three technologies were tried: steam, cables, and, finally, electric traction. By this time steam was no longer new; steam railroads had existed since early in the nineteenth century. In 1870 a steam-operated urban rail line was opened in New York on an elevated track. Although other lines were later opened in New York and elsewhere, steam power faced strong opposition from municipal leaders because of the noise, dirt, and perceived danger of steam-powered vehicles.[16] In Great Britain a steam-powered omnibus had been successfully used in intercity service. There, too, however, the public distrust of steam was strong, and in 1865 the "red flag" law was passed. This law limited the vehicles to four miles per hour and required that each vehicle be preceded by a man on foot with a red flag. The law was finally repealed in 1896 by the Locomotives on the Highways Act.[17]

In 1873, the first cable car, or "grip car," as it was known in those days, began operating in San Francisco. The cable car had been made possible by Andrew Hallidie's invention in 1869 of a grip that allowed the car to be linked to a continuously moving cable.[18] The speed of a cable car was about ten miles per hour, an appreciable increase over the horsecar.[19] Chicago, New York, and Philadelphia soon had cable cars, and by the mid-1890s 626 miles of cable car lines existed in the country.[20] However, high installation costs and frequent breakdowns prevented the cable car from becoming a dominant mode of urban travel.

What did become dominant, of course, was the electric streetcar, or trolley. The world's first electric streetcar had been tested in Berlin in 1881, five years before Frank Sprague tested the first streetcar in the United States in Montgomery, Alabama. In 1887, Sprague built the first streetcar system, a twelve-mile line in Richmond, Virginia, and within thirteen years there were 850 streetcar systems with ten thousand miles of line.[21] In the twelve years after 1890, urban rail networks in the United States, which had been 69.7 percent horse operated, became 97 percent electric powered.[22] The age of the horse had come to an end.

The streetcar was introduced at a crucial time in the development of American cities. At a time of great urbanization the speeds of a streetcar—over ten miles per hour—provided the means by which persons could commute long distances, thereby allowing the cities, which had been becoming denser, to expand. The importance of the streetcar in urban growth has been carefully documented by Warner in his study of Boston.[23] Glaab and Brown suggest that the streetcar may have prevented an independent metropolis from emerging north of New York City by allowing persons in that area to commute to lower Manhattan.[24] These and other researchers have supported the thesis that increasing travel speeds made possible a more dispersed urban settlement pattern.

A somewhat different view was put forth by Weber in 1898.[25] Based upon the 1890 census, Weber reported that the annual number of trips by street rail—horsecar and streetcar—was much greater in American cities than in European cities. For example, Berlin, "with the best street railways system in Europe," had eighty-seven rides per capita per year, a figure which placed it twenty-second among cities in the United States. He used those figures to argue that suburbanization had occurred well *before* the arrival of the electric streetcar and stated: "It should rather be said that the American penchant for dwelling in cottage homes instead of business blocks after the fashion of Europe is the cause, and the trolley the effect."[26]

Regardless of whether it was the "cause" or the "effect," the streetcar supported the spread of urban areas. It also dominated mass transit until the 1920s. Perhaps more important, however, the streetcar produced a new transit management structure: the city-wide firm. As Smerk has pointed out, the high fixed costs of streetcar development meant that there were economies of scale in larger operating systems. Competing firms were soon forced by the new economic realities to merge into single city-wide firms, often owned by the local power utility. This trend toward monopoly transit operations marked a significant change from the highly competitive conditions that had always existed in the mass transit industry, a change which is still manifested in regional transit authorities.

## THE BIRTH OF THE AUTOMOBILE

The technological advances of the later 1800s—which revolutionized the fixed-route transit industry—had a comparable impact on the paratransit industry. There it was development of the automobile, rather than the electric streetcar, which created the revolution.

The search for a replacement for the horse led to experimental vehicles using steam, electricity, and various types of gasoline engines.[27] Much of this experimentation was done initially in Europe. As Rae has succinctly stated: "The automobile is European by birth, American by adoption."[28]

The first steam-powered car was built by Nicholas Cugnot in France in 1796. Actually, the Cugnot vehicle was hardly a car but rather a clumsy three-wheeled carriage designed to pull a cannon. Later, during the 1890s, inventors in both Europe and America were able to reduce the weight of steam engines by using higher pressure steam. In 1897 steam-powered cars were commercially produced for the first time by Francis and Freelan Stanley. The "Stanley Steamer" was manufactured by the Stanley brothers until Francis died in 1918. By the 1920s other manufacturers had also given up on the steam-powered car.

As Rae points out, there were several reasons for the failure of the steamer. One was the nagging fear of boiler explosions. Another was the need for constant maintenance and water supplies. The steamer's fate was sealed in 1912 when Charles Kettering developed the electric starter, thereby solving one of the main problems of the steamer's main competitor, the gasoline engine car.

The electric car was also an early competitor in the race to develop a self-propelled vehicle. In 1891, William Morrison developed the first electric vehicle in the United States in Des Moines, Iowa. In 1894, Henry Morris and Pedro Salom began commercial production of an electric vehicle when they introduced their Electrobat, which was built as a taxicab. Their Electric Storage Battery Company, which later became the Electric Vehicle Company, began to build electric vehicles before the turn of the century; however, the problem of the heavy batteries was one that the electric vehicle would never overcome. By

1910 the electric vehicle had been eclipsed by the steamer and the gasoline automobile.

The internal combustion engine vehicle dates back to 1860 when Etienne Lenoir patented a two-cycle engine in Paris. Later, in 1878, Nikolaus Otto built the first four-cycle engine. In the years that followed a number of inventors in both Europe and America began experimenting with a variety of engine designs.

According to Rae, however, the eventual winner—the four-cycle, spark-ignition gasoline engine—can be traced to two Germans. In 1885, Karl Benz and Gottlieb Daimler built vehicles that greatly influenced the evolution of the automobile industry. Benz constructed a tricycle that used a spark-ignition gasoline engine, while Daimler built a high-speed engine and mounted it on a motorcycle. Seven years later yet another important engine was developed when Rudolph Diesel patented the compression-ignition internal combustion engine. The "diesel" engine was later sold to Adolphus Busch of St. Louis.

In the United States, Charles and Frank Duryea read of Benz's vehicle and built their own version in 1893. However, the Duryeas would not reap the fame for developing the automobile. Instead, Henry Ford, Ransom Olds, David Buick, Alexander Winton, James Packard, John and Henry Dodge, and others seized on the commercial potential of the "horseless carriage" and began production of the automobile.

The success of the automobile was almost immediate. Ford built his first automobile, the "quadricycle," in 1896; in 1908, he built 5,986 vehicles. Five years later Ford production hit 182,809, and in 1916 it reached 577,036.[29] This Ford car, the Model T, cost $850 in 1908 and only $360 in 1916. The total automobile production and registration during these early years is shown in Table 3.2.

## THE BIRTH OF THE TAXICAB

Like the various mass transit modes, the taxicab is a descendant of the hackney, the horse-drawn vehicle that flourished until the early 1800s. By late in the nineteenth century both the cabriolet and the hansom had been developed in Europe, and the terms *hansom cab, hansom,* and

TABLE 3.2. *Early Automobile Production and Registration*

| Year | Automobile Production | Automobile Registration |
|---|---|---|
| 1900 | 4,192 | 8,000 |
| 1902 | 9,000 | 23,000 |
| 1904 | 22,130 | 54,590 |
| 1906 | 33,200 | 105,900 |
| 1908 | 63,500 | 194,000 |
| 1910 | 181,000 | 458,377 |
| 1912 | 356,000 | 901,596 |
| 1914 | 548,139 | 1,644,003 |

Source: Motor Vehicles Manufacturers Association, *Facts and Figures*, 1972.

*cab* were used to describe paratransit services in both America and Europe.

However, the paratransit industry was quickly affected by—and in turn influenced—the development of the automobile. During the last several years of the nineteenth century three motorized cabs were built: the Benz in Stuttgart, the Roger-Benz in Paris, and the Electrobat in Philadelphia. Interest in motorized cabs flourished during this time; a Paris competition in 1898 for motorized cabs attracted thirteen electric cabs and one gasoline cab.

The first electric cab in America was the Salom's Electrobat. This vehicle was a hansom cab with a battery mounted on the rear below the driver's seat. Later, however, the driver's seat was moved to the front in order to improve the balance of the vehicle. These strange-looking vehicles must have created a stir in New York streets when in 1897 the Electric Carriage and Wagon Company placed twelve electric cabs in service.[30] Passengers rode in the front, with the driver atop the rear of the vehicle. The batteries, which weighed eight hundred to nine hundred pounds, had to be frequently changed and recharged. The maximum speed was fifteen miles per hour, and recharging took eight hours. Parts had short lives, and electricity to recharge the batteries was expensive and limited. The weight of the vehicles proved too much for the pneumatic tires, which had only recently been developed. A writer of the time, H. C. Moore, reported that "while you meet hundreds of people who have had one ride in an electric cab, you come across very few who have had two. It is not because their experience was unpleasant that they have not had a second one, but it was not so enjoyable as a ride in a horse-drawn cab. Apparently the hansom cab has every prospect of retaining its popularity for another sixty years."[31]

Despite these problems, the New York electric cab fleet was expanded to 62 cabs in 1898 and 100 in 1899. However, the manufacturer of the vehicle, the Electric Vehicle Company, suffered as the electric vehicle was overtaken by the gasoline automobile. The company manufactured only about 2,000 electric cabs before ceasing production soon after the turn of the century. In New York the fate of the electric hansom cab was abruptly decided in 1907 when a fire destroyed 300 of the 750 electric cabs owned by the Electric Carriage and Wagon Company.[32]

With the demise of the electric cab, the horse-drawn hansoms—and, in London, the "growlers"—enjoyed a period of unchallenged superiority. In fact, in London, the number of horse-drawn cabs peaked early in the twentieth century; in 1901 London had 11,252 cabs licensed, of which 7,531 were two-wheelers and the rest four-wheelers. There were 13,201 cab drivers and 2,782 proprietors. However, this period of horse-drawn superiority was not to last long.

In 1907 a New York man was taking a lady friend home from a Manhattan restaurant. Halting a hansom cab, the couple rode a distance of about three-fourths of a mile, whereupon they were charged five dollars. This event so angered the man that he vowed to set up a new cab service, one which would charge low rates based upon the distance traveled. The man was Harry N. Allen, and he was thirty years old.

On October 1 of that year Allen fulfilled his vow. Borrowing three million dollars, two of which were from European backers, Allen introduced sixty-five new cabs to the streets of New York. These were not the conventional cabs; they were shiny, red, gasoline-powered

Darracq automobiles, which Allen imported from France. Acquiring cab stands at all the major hotels, Allen quickly prospered and soon had seven hundred cabs on the streets. On the first anniversary of his new cab service, his drivers began a bloody seven-week strike, which apparently cooled Allen's interest in the cab business. Within a year he had left the business, and he spent the rest of his business career importing cars.[33]

However, Allen left to the world a new word: *taxicab*. He called his new firm the New York Taxicab Association because his vehicles were equipped with a distance-measuring device which the French called "taxi-mètre," meaning a meter for measuring the fare or tax. The French, however, had not invented the taximeter; that honor belongs to Wilhelm Bruhn, who had invented it in Germany in 1891. Unlike earlier such devices, Bruhn's taximeter was mechanical and measured both time and distance. It was first tried in a few Berlin cabs, where it met with formidable resistance from drivers and cab owners alike. However, the riding public was so enthusiastic about the prospect of not being cheated that many passengers went out of their way to hire cabs equipped with taximeters. This popularity overcame all resistance, and soon fifty-five hundred of Berlin's eight thousand cabs had taximeters.

The use of taximeters soon spread to other European cities. In 1899 six London cabs were fitted with taximeters on a trial basis. The Cab Drivers' Union strongly opposed the experiment, however, and soon succeeded in having the meters removed. Yet, by 1906 the taximeter was in use in London and most other European cities. When Allen introduced the taximeter along with his new motorized cabs in New York in 1907, the names *taxicab* and *taxi* soon evolved to describe this new paratransit service.

But the taxicab was more than just a new word. It represented a new, faster, more convenient form of personal urban transportation. Just as the electric streetcar had supplanted the omnibus and the horsecar, the taxicab quickly dispatched the horse-drawn hansom to be but an artifact of a prior age. Soon the paratransit industry was entirely dependent on the internal combustion engine. After centuries of reliance on horse-drawn vehicles, the development and testing

*Early electric hansom cab in New York City. (From* Scientific American, *March 13, 1897, used by permission.)*

*Electric hansom cab in New York City getting a recharged battery installed. The weight of the battery necessitated the large tires. (From* Scientific American, *March 25, 1899, used by permission.)*

of new mechanized vehicles and the selection of the internal combustion engine automobile occurred with remarkable speed and without governmental finances—or regulations.

One of the consequences of this technological change was seen in an event which occurred many thousands of miles away in France. Throughout August 1915 the German army swept through western Europe in a scythelike movement toward Paris, eventually to a front stabilized at three tributaries of the Marne River: the Ourcq, the Petit Morin, and the Grand Morin. On both sides strategy was argued amid general confusion. A mix-up of signals resulted in a counterattack by General Manoury and the French Sixth Army at the Ourcq two days early! He was blocked by the German Third and Fourth Corps, and his army began to crumble. He called for help.

It was at this time that an otherwise little-known general achieved fame. General Gallieni had been placed in command of the Paris garrison when the French government had precipitously fled Paris. He took seriously his responsibility to defend Paris, and as a result of his action every Frenchman remembers him and the taxicabs of Paris. General Gallieni gathered together the twelve hundred taxicabs of Paris, loaded them with soldiers from the garrison, and proceeded to the rescue of the Sixth Army. Whether or not this event was the critical move that resulted in the victory at the Marne is not at all certain, but it is remembered as the "Miracle of the Marne," and it gave the taxicabs of Paris a special place in history as well as in the hearts of Frenchmen.

# 4

# THE BIRTH OF TAXICAB FLEETS

## WAR AND PROSPERITY

The infant taxi industry had a lot of growing to do after World War I ended. It had been undergoing a transition from horse power to gasoline engines before and during the war years. Still, it was an industry that comprised many small firms and independent owner-operators. It lagged behind the streetcar industry, which had electrified in the 1890s and was consolidating into large city-wide firms early in the new century.

Conditions after World War I were conducive to the economic growth of many industries, including the taxi industry. Urbanization continued, and the country became officially "urban" for the first time in 1920, when 50.9 percent of the population lived in urban places. By 1920 three cities could boast more than a million residents and sixty-eight had over one hundred thousand. Ten years later, ninety-three cities had one hundred thousand residents. Congress had enacted control to restrict the number of immigrants, but the urban centers continued to grow from internal migration from rural areas. Everywhere cities were busy building schools, streets, electrical systems, and water and sewer systems. The city planning profession, born in the "City Beautiful" movement around 1910, matured into a concern with making the city function well, a concern labeled the "City Efficient" movement. Zoning, first tried in New York in 1916, spread quickly; by 1926 there were 564 cities with zoning ordinances.[1]

It was also a time of prosperity and inflation. Between 1915 and 1920 the consumer price index almost doubled. Still, real income rose during those five years by 7 percent. During the 1920s the consumer price index actually decreased, producing real income increases of 12 percent for 1920–25 and 10 percent for 1925–30. The increased personal wealth, coupled with new technological advances, spurred the rapid adoption of consumer conveniences such as telephones, electric lights, bathtubs, and, certainly, the automobile. Between 1910 and 1920 the number of persons per vehicle in the United States dropped from 120.9 to only 7.7. By 1930 five million automobiles were being produced annually, and every person who had invested twenty-five thousand dollars in General Motors in 1921 was a millionaire.

These three decades brought other fundamental transportation changes, the results of which still persist. The federal involvement in highway building began in 1916, the same year that railroads, interurbans, and streetcars all reached their peak numbers of miles of track. The railroad was challenged by the truck as a freight carrier; the urban streetcar was largely replaced by the bus; and the interurban streetcar came and went.

## THE EVOLUTION OF TAXI FLEETS

The bustling years from 1915 to 1930 were important years of change for the taxicab industry. The automobile had replaced the horse, and the telephone had become a commonplace, albeit important, element of taxicab operations. Most important, however, was the emergence of enterprising individuals who organized the taxicab industry, which had previously been composed of many small firms and individual owner-operators, into large fleets. This development produced a new level of service and a source of innovation within the industry.

Throughout the country in the early 1920s individual entrepreneurs were expanding their taxi fleets and purchasing their competitors. Products of a time of enormous economic opportunity, many of these entrepreneurs, in true Horatio Alger fashion, grew from very poor beginnings to become prosperous businessmen. A closer examination of four of these men—John Hertz, Morris Markin, W. Lansing Rothschild, and Frank Sawyer—will provide important insights into the development of the new industry as well as of the climate of economic opportunity that existed in the 1920s.

# 40 / The Taxicab

## JOHN D. HERTZ

While John D. Hertz is best remembered for the car rental company that bears his name, that enterprise was perhaps the least of his accomplishments. He was in later years a financier and a successful racehorse owner. His major accomplishment, however, was developing the world's largest taxicab company.

Hertz was born in 1879 in Ruttka, an Austrian village which is now a part of Czechoslovakia, but he came to Chicago at an early age. He finished fifth grade in school and then ran away from home at age eleven. Life was not easy for Hertz. He stayed in a waif's home and paid $2 per week for room and board while he worked as a copyboy for a newspaper at $2.50 per week. He worked at the newspaper at night for three years until he was fired because he was too frail. Ironically, he then became a truck driver at age fifteen. To build himself physically he spent $10 for a series of boxing lessons, which led to a few exhibition fights. The interest in boxing extended to writing stories for the *Chicago Record* at $.25 per inch, then to a job as sports writer and later assistant sports editor, at which point he gave up truck driving. His pay varied from $3,000 to $5,000, and he must have felt proud of his success. However, he lost his job when the newspaper was merged into another. He managed two boxers until his fiancée's family objected and a friend induced him to sell automobiles. It was 1904; he was twenty-six years old and had never been in an automobile!

After a slow start, Hertz became fantastically successful as a car salesman. After earning less than $900 his first year, Hertz applied for the vacant job of manager of the local automobile agency. The $50-per-week salary plus commission was very tempting to him, but he was rejected. In spite he promised the company president that the next year he would earn more than the manager. He did; his 5 percent commission yielded him $12,000. His success was largely attributable to his well-known honesty and to his practice of providing emergency road repair service to any of his customers at any hour of the day. After earning $13,000 his third year, he quit, partly because the automobile company was faltering economically.

Hertz then entered business on his own, along with Walden W.

Shaw, who had an agency selling French automobiles. For $2,000 he purchased one-fourth interest in Shaw's financially troubled agency, which was $45,000 in the red. The next year the agency grossed $500,000, of which Hertz sold $385,000, and he netted $90,000. Much of this surplus was in the form of traded-in cars—a new problem for the infant automobile dealerships. Hertz's response was to put the second-hand cars to work as taxicabs. Thus, by chance, Hertz became a taxi operator.

Hertz and Shaw entered the taxicab business in 1907, and they continued with it until 1915, with Hertz as the general manager. He proved to be very farsighted. Determined to avoid a repetition of a debilitating strike, he made his drivers partners (via a profit-sharing plan involving 20 percent of profits) and paid them a commission. In the years to follow he installed a doctor, a dentist, and a nurse in the company's main office building. The nurse would make house calls on those unable to come to the office. The "house attorneys" working at the office were available to assist employees in difficulties. Hertz also "forced" his employees to save at least five dollars per week by maintaining savings accounts for those employees who could not save on their own. He insisted that his drivers do no car repairs, partly because he wanted only specialized mechanics to tinker with his vehicles.

If his concepts of management-labor relations were radical, his ideas of taxicab service were revolutionary. The infant taxi industry had become a service for the rich; rates had risen to $.70 for the first mile, $.40 per mile thereafter, or $5 per hour. Soon after entering the taxi business, Hertz slashed the rates to $.30 per mile or $2.50 per hour. He also stopped charging for deadhead mileage to or from a pickup point, and he advertised that he could have a cab at anyone's home within ten minutes. His competition was sure that his fare cuts would push him into bankruptcy, but he further amazed them by cutting fares to $.20 per mile. Taxicabs became a service for the nonrich as well as the rich.

Hertz also believed that successful taxicab service depended on the quality of the drivers. Hertz insisted that the drivers be neatly dressed in a uniform that included a hat and well-shined shoes and puttees. To promote this good appearance, he hired a tailor and stationed him in the main office. Before beginning work, each driver was required to present himself to the dispatcher with his uniform in proper condition and with a whisk broom, which the drivers used to sweep the cab after each load, and, in winter, a wool lap robe for the passengers' comfort.

Aware of the need to maximize the usage of his vehicles, Hertz revolutionized the way in which taxis operated. After reading a University of Chicago study that found yellow (with a slight tint of red) to be the most visible color at the greatest distances, he painted his taxis yellow. He installed a network of telephone dispatching (at one time the largest telephone system in Chicago) so that drivers could stand at garages and company-owned lots, private stands at hotels, clubs, and railroad stations, and public stands, where he had affixed telephones to nearby walls. This system not only decreased the deadheading back to the "Loop" but also made the cabs available for service sooner. Incidentally, this system also broke the hold of hotels on taxicab stands. One Chicago hotel, for example, had previously charged twenty thousand dollars annually for its taxicab stand.

Among his other advanced notions were stop-and-go lights for boulevards, which he believed would speed up traffic and thus get his cabs more quickly to their destinations. To induce the city of Chicago to install them, he put them in along Michigan Boulevard from Twelfth Street north to Randolph Street (a distance of about one and a half miles), with towers at each end and one in the middle to house the operators. The agreement was that Hertz would pay for the installation and remove it if the city did not like it; otherwise, he would be reimbursed. The system was an instant success.

In his early years as a taxi operator, Hertz tried many makes of automobiles. None was made especially to be a taxi, and all were subject to frequent repairs. Hertz got a parts catalog and priced out the cost of a new taxicab which, unlike existing taxicabs, would be a built-for-the-purpose taxi. He immediately decided to produce his own cabs. In 1915 he manufactured his first taxicab, and on 1 December of that year the Yellow Cab Company was incorporated to operate and manufacture taxicabs. A short time later the Yellow Cab Manufacturing Company was organized to take over the production of the taxis.

Both companies were extremely successful. Yellow Cab expanded from forty taxis in 1915, to six hundred in 1918, and to twenty-seven hundred in 1925, and became the largest taxi company in the world. Hertz helped organize Yellow Cab companies, as well as Black and White Cab companies, in other cities, including Kansas City, Philadelphia, and New York. He soon discovered, however, that without his personal attention they did not flourish, and he sold them all to local entrepreneurs.

Yellow Cab Manufacturing Company also prospered. It sold cabs to many taxi firms, including Hertz's affiliates in other cities and, of course, to Yellow Cab Company. Soon Yellow Cab Manufacturing expanded into bus manufacturing and later into the production of trucks. It acquired the R.&V. Motor Company to assure a supply of engines for its buses. A perhaps apocryphal account states that Hertz also purchased a company with patents on a gearless transmission for a hybrid gasoline electric motor, but this purchase does not seem to have been documented. He took over the defunct Chicago Motor Coach Company, raided Fifth Avenue Coach of John A. Ritchie, its president and operator, and Colonel George A. Green, its designer, and moved them into Yellow's plant. The company provided 420 buses for Chicago, 90 for People's Motorbus of St. Louis, and 80 for Fifth Avenue Coach. In 1924 and 1925 Public Service Corporation of New Jersey bought 500 (at a cost of $5 million) and Philadelphia Rapid Transit bought 579 ($6.5 million).

On 2 September 1919, Yellow Cab Company entered into a contract with Firestone Tire & Rubber Company for the lease of tires to be used by Yellow Cabs, to be paid for on the basis of miles traveled. Firestone was to maintain and repair them. With the exception of one short period that relationship has continued to the present, and the world's largest taxicab fleet has never owned a tire! During the early years of the arrangement the spare tire was carried on the rear of the cab and the word *Firestone* impressed into the sidewall was hand painted in silver. The mounted tires were whitewashed on the sidewalls before each shift—the forerunner of whitewalls. Later, the tires proved so reliable that it was cheaper to dispatch a tow truck to change a flat tire than to carry a spare (particularly since Hertz was firmly opposed to having his drivers do any mechanical work whatsoever). When Firestone developed the "balloon" tire, Hertz was so sure of its value that he bought new wheels with wide rims for all of his cabs in order to use the new tire. The narrow tires were never used again.

On the early taxicabs the windshields were divided in half horizontally, and in inclement weather the driver swiveled the upper half into a horizontal position so that he could see forward. (There were no side windows.) Yellow Cab developed a hand-operated windshield wiper for the upper portion of the window, and soon thereafter installed the first automatic windshield wipers.

A quirk of fate brought Hertz into the industry which was to make his name a household word. In 1918, Walter Jacobs was a salesman in a Ford dealership in Chicago. Unsatisfied with his small earnings, Jacobs decided to go into the used car business. Like other car dealers, he rented out his unsold cars by the day.[2] Realizing the potential of the rental business, Jacobs soon left the used car business and entered the car rental business, beginning with twelve used Ford Model T cars.

Jacobs's new venture became a prosperous one, but not without much hard work. Having no money for advertising, he sent handwritten penny postcards to persons and firms appearing in the telephone yellow pages. Another firm in the car rental field, the Saunders System, had already opened car rental branches in many cities, but perhaps because of a too rapid expansion many branches failed. Acquiring these defunct branches while expanding his own operations, Jacobs increased his fleet to some six hundred cars.

In 1923, Alfred Foreman of the Foreman Bank and Trust Company in Chicago suggested to Hertz that he try to purchase Jacobs's car rental business as a means of creating a market for the "Ambassador," a modified taxicab which the Yellow Cab Manufacturing Company was manufacturing. Hertz, who conceived the idea that a rental car should be rugged, agreed and soon bought Jacobs's business, bringing Jacobs along to operate it. Hertz then modified the Ambassador and named it the "Hertz," and introduced it as a rental car in 1924 in the Yellow Drive-It-Yourself Company.

According to Jacobs, Hertz's introduction of the modified taxicab as a rental car was a mistake. While Hertz had been correct in assuming that taxi passengers wanted to ride in a clearly defined taxi ve-

*Typical taxicab in Chicago at the time of World War I. (Collection of the author.)*

*Central control tower of the first traffic light system, Michigan Avenue at Jackson Boulevard in Chicago. The operator stood in the tower and controlled the traffic lights. The double-decked bus in the foreground was manufactured by Yellow Cab Manufacturing Company. (Collection of the author.)*

*A taxicab of the 1920s with convertible rear roof. The driver rode in an open compartment but did have a two-part windshield. The box on the running board contains the battery. (Collection of the author.)*

*A Chicago Yellow Cab of the 1920s with the driver in his winter uniform. Tire chains were installed whenever it rained. (Collection of the author.)*

*Chicago Yellow Cab driver trainees being taught the proper way to crank an engine. Training took about two weeks. Drivers were expected to maintain their uniforms and shine their shoes each day. (Collection of the author.)*

hicle, which is why he had painted his taxis yellow, he could not understand why car rental customers did not want to be seen driving a vehicle that, because of its distinct similarity to a taxicab, was marked as a rented rather than an owned vehicle. Hertz was dismayed to find that car rental customers would rent the Hertz vehicle only when no other kind of vehicle was available.

One year later, in 1925, Hertz began withdrawing from the taxicab business. His reasons for doing so are not known; he was 46 and had been in the taxi business for eighteen years. Perhaps he was looking for a new challenge, for he did move into new endeavors. Perhaps he was discouraged that his Hertz cars had proved so unpopular with his car rental customers. In July of that year he sold Yellow Cab Manufacturing Company to General Motors, and threw in the Yellow Drive-It-Yourself System as part of the package.

The deal provided Hertz with the funds he needed to expand his Omnibus Corporation, which owned several transit systems, including Chicago Motor Coach and Fifth Avenue Coach in New York. Four years later Hertz sold Yellow Cab Company to the Parmelee System, which in turn was soon purchased by Checker Motors. Upon leaving Yellow Cab, Hertz distributed $250,000 among sixty of his longtime Yellow Cab employees.

For General Motors the deal produced mixed results. Accounts vary as to why General Motors purchased Yellow Cab Manufacturing and Yellow Drive-It-Yourself. One account claims that GM wanted the patent rights to certain components that Yellow Cab Manufacturing had developed for buses and trucks. Whatever the reason, it is clear that GM had little interest in either the taxicab manufacturing or the car rental activities. It made Yellow Cab Manufacturing a new GM division, the Yellow Truck and Coach Division, and did little with the rental car business. In 1953 GM sold Yellow Drive-It-Yourself for $10.8 million to Hertz's Omnibus Corporation, which by that time had wisely divested itself of its mass transit holdings. Omnibus Corporation promptly changed its name to Hertz Rent-a-Car.

General Motors would have been wise to ignore the taxicab business as well. One account states that GM tried to sell the taxicab portion of Yellow Cab Manufacturing to Checker Motors in the late 1920s.[3] Checker inferred from the GM offer that GM was not interested in producing taxis and declined the offer, preferring instead to await the death of the division. Instead of letting the division disappear, GM continued production and decided to compete vigorously with Checker. The Parmelee Transportation Company, which operated taxis in New York and several other cities, had been closely aligned with Yellow Cab Manufacturing since 1919 and had always purchased Yellow taxis. In 1928, just prior to its purchase by Checker Motors, Parmelee began purchasing its vehicles from Checker. In retaliation, GM started its own New York taxi operating firm, Terminal Taxi. In two separate ventures and with Grand Central Station as its exclusive cab stand, General Motors lost nearly $2 million on Terminal Taxi and finally gave up manufacturing taxicabs.[4]

For Hertz, the GM-Checker rivalry was of little consequence; he had all but left the transportation business. In 1934 he joined Lehman Brothers investment firm while retaining financial involvement in the Omnibus Corporation. He was an active racehorse breeder and owner and owned Reigh Count, a winner of the Kentucky Derby. After serving on the board of directors of Hertz Rent-a-Car for one year, Hertz retired in 1955. He died in 1961.

### MORRIS MARKIN

A second pioneer of the taxicab industry was Morris Markin. Born in 1893 in Smolensk, a city in western Russia, Markin worked in a clothing factory during his young years and rose to be a supervisor by age nineteen, when he emigrated to the United States. He arrived at Ellis Island unable to speak English and without enough money to pay the bond required to enter the country. An Ellis Island janitor loaned him the twenty-five dollars for the bond.

He went to Chicago, where an uncle lived, and held several jobs as an errand boy, the last for a tailor who taught him the trade. When the tailor died, Markin bought the business from the widow (on credit) and went into the tailoring business. He saved enough money to bring seven brothers and two sisters to the United States. With one of those brothers, Markin opened a pants factory which made pants under government contracts during World War I and prospered afterward.

In 1921 an automobile body engineer by the name of Lomberg approached Markin for a fifteen-thousand-dollar loan to finance his struggling auto body manufacturing business. In those days bodies were made of wood with canvas tops. Unable to make the business go, Lomberg returned to Markin for more money, but Markin refused and took over the company for his debt. At about the same time Commonwealth Motors, a small independent automobile manufacturer with contracts for chassis, was also in financial difficulty. During 1920 its accountant, Ralph E. Oakland, had conceived of the idea of discounting sixty-day trade acceptances (it took only thirty days to manufacture a chassis) and used this device to sell stock to the public.[5] This strategy failed, however, and Markin purchased the defunct company. Oakland came with the deal and remained as Markin's financial adviser until Markin's death in 1970.

In 1922, Markin made a bold move. Purchasing the defunct Hadley-Knight chassis plant in Kalamazoo, as well as the Dort body plant, he moved his entire manufacturing operation to Kalamazoo and on 2 February 1922 formed the Checker Cab Manufacturing Company. With him came Oakland and Henry Weiss, who had been a New York distributor for Commonwealth Motors and who became Checker's first distributor in New York City. According to Oakland, Markin—despite his close involvement with Checker—knew little about the taxi manufacturing process and visited the Kalamazoo factory only a few days each year until he moved to Kalamazoo in 1943.[6]

Taxicab manufacturing was a very competitive industry in the 1920s and early 1930s. Many automobile makes were modified into taxicabs over the years. In fact, from 1925 to 1928 no fewer than twenty-five brands of cars were used as taxis in New York City alone. However, the stress and wear of continual city operation was too much for all but a handful of these car makes. In addition to Yellow and Checker—the only makes built specifically as taxicabs—only three brands of cars lasted very long in the New York market: General Motors, Paramount, and Dodge. Several automobile companies made sporadic attempts to enter the taxicab manufacturing business, such as Ford in 1928 and 1929 and General Motors' General Cab in 1936 and 1938. Finally, though, after Yellow Cab joined General Motors, only Checker and DeSoto (modified for New York City) remained as manufacturers of specially built taxis. Both produced large, heavy, comfortable vehicles able to absorb much abuse. This was to pay off during World War II. When the manufacture of taxicabs was suspended, operators were able to "make do" with their old Checkers and DeSotos until the war was over, at which time DeSoto withdrew from the taxi manufacturing industry.

Given this competitive market, it was logical that Markin would seek to control taxi operating firms in various cities so as to assure a market for new Checker vehicles. In 1929 he organized the National Transportation Company in New York City, a firm which eventually operated fifteen hundred taxis in that city. In that same year he acquired Chicago Yellow Cab Company, partially from Hertz and partially by purchasing the Parmelee Transportation Company, which had already purchased 30 percent of Chicago Yellow.

The Parmelee purchase was a bold and interesting acquisition. Parmelee had been started in 1863 by Frank Parmelee, a thirty-seven-year-old entrepreneur who had arrived in Chicago with an idea for a new business venture. Chicago was a growing rail center of thirty thousand population. Unfortunately for rail passengers, the various railroads serving Chicago had elected to build separate rail terminals, and six major railroad stations were located near the Loop. Parmelee's idea was to transfer rail passengers and their luggage from one terminal to another and to and from the downtown hotels.

He started with six omnibus vehicles and quickly prospered. The concept was a simple one. When passengers purchased their rail tickets, they received a coupon for free transfer between rail stations. Thus, the railroads, not the passengers, paid for the Parmelee service. Parmelee diversified into horse-drawn streetcars between 1858 and 1863, but his main interest remained the railroad transfer business. In 1903, one year before his death, Parmelee sold his firm to a syndicate made up of Marshall Field and other prominent Chicago residents.[7]

When Markin purchased Parmelee Transportation in 1929, it had seventy-six years of urban transportation experience. For the preceding ten of those years, Parmelee had been owned by Charles A. McCulloch, chairman of the board of Chicago Yellow Cab, and Parmelee had purchased 30 percent of Chicago Yellow. Markin also bought Yellow Cab Company of Pittsburg and Yellow Taxi Company of Minneapolis and included them, along with the National Transportation Company in New York City, in the Parmelee Company. He kept the New York operation until 1954, when he began selling his fifteen hundred New York City medallions.

Markin also expanded in the Chicago taxicab industry. Chicago Yellow Cab Company was a holding company which owned Yellow Cab Company, the largest taxicab company in the world, its own insurance company, and its own maintenance facility. Under Hertz, Chicago Yellow Cab had gone public, with Hertz, Parmelee, and the public owning about equal shares. Hertz had sold his stock to Markin when he left the industry, and in the acquisition of Parmelee, Markin obtained control of its share of Chicago Yellow Cab. Eventually, in

1963, Chicago Yellow Cab was merged into Checker Motors Corporation, and Yellow Cab Company became a wholly owned subsidiary of Checker Motors. However, when Markin obtained Yellow, there was still a major taxi competitor in Chicago: Checker Taxi Company.

Checker was an association of independent owner-operators organized by Frank Dilger of Oak Park. This association had selected the "checker" logo and had given Markin contracts to build cabs. Always in a turmoil of dissent, the association was changing from one of individual owner-operators to one of some individuals plus groups of entrepreneurs who owned several or even as many as twenty-five taxicabs. Some of these entrepreneurs were very rough people who contested among themselves for territories and privileges. Frank Sawyer, owner of Checker Cab Company in Boston, recounts his trip to Chicago to buy into the association and his hasty departure when he realized the caliber of the owners and their vicious internal situation. His decision to leave without purchasing Checker was an easy one, particularly after he peered into a closet at Checker and found it full of firearms![8]

It was the Depression which brought Markin to Checker Taxi. Markin was owed a great deal of money for cabs purchased by Checker Taxi, and Checker Taxi, an association, was in turn owed a great amount of money from its members for dues, garaging, and maintenance. Everyone owed for insurance premiums. Markin, Oakland, and two associates, Paul Lamoreaux and Ernest Miller, decided to purchase Checker Taxi. As an association, Checker Taxi consisted of assets owned by the many association members. Rather than negotiate with each owner individually, Oakland suggested that they organize their own company to operate within the association; this they did, starting with thirty-five repossessed and rebuilt Checker cabs. Their fleet increased, and the independents continued to go by the boards. In 1935 they approached Michael Sokoll, secretary of the association (who had sold insurance to the independents and had money coming also), to operate Checker Taxi for the four partners. He did so for many years until his death. Ultimately, the few remaining independents were bought out, and Checker Taxi became the third (and later the second) largest fleet in the country, finally wholly owned by Markin personally.

In 1970, Morris Markin died. He left behind the only taxicab manufacturing company and the largest taxicab operation in the country.

### W. LANSING ROTHSCHILD

In partnership with Al Baldi, W. Lansing Rothschild operated a cigar store in the St. Francis Hotel in San Francisco.[9] Baldi made the cigars, and Rothschild sold them. A taxicab parked across the street every day, waiting for business. The owner of the taxi was having marital difficulties because he did not come home in the evenings after work. His wife suspected that he had other female companions and told him that if he did not get rid of the cab, she would leave. Unable to find a buyer, he asked Rothschild to help. Rothschild bought the business for $800 in 1916. He had expanded to fourteen cabs in 1922 when Charles Davis came to the city representing Checker Motors. Davis wanted Rothschild to purchase a Checker franchise and some Checker taxicabs. By then firmly entrenched in the taxi business, Rothschild saw the wisdom of such an investment. He purchased the franchise and twenty Checker taxis for $250,000, and on 17 January 1923 he organized the Checker Cab Company.

One of Rothschild's wisest moves was to hire John Pettit, who had worked for Yellow Cab of San Francisco for a year as a service salesman. When the Yellow Cab drivers went on strike, Pettit joined Rothschild's Checker Cab. A few months later, he undertook, at his own expense, a ten-thousand-mile trip to visit the leading twenty-two cab companies in Chicago, Denver, Cleveland, Pittsburgh, Washington, and twelve other cities. Pettit wrote daily reports back to Rothschild on maintenance procedures, the value of whitewashing tires, vehicle cleanliness, and other aspects of the taxi business. Pettit was most impressed with the advantages of yellow cabs and the importance of marketing taxi services. Returning to San Francisco well-versed in Hertz's public relations methods, he sold Rothschild on the idea of cutting fares to promote ridership. Like Hertz, Pettit believed in making the drivers feel a part of the company, and he sold eighty-five thousand dollars worth of Checker stock to the drivers in his first three years. He was put in charge of training, hiring, and public relations, and later he advanced to general manager and vice-president.

Rothschild's success in the taxi business soon prompted him to expand further. He purchased Yellow Cab of San Francisco from A. O. Smith, who went to Los Angeles to operate the Yellow Cab there. Rothschild used Yellow Cab of San Francisco as an umbrella for expanding into other cities. At one time he operated taxi firms in fourteen California cities, plus Yellow Cab of Phoenix, several bus companies, and a small airline. These operations were later merged into the Yellow Cab Company of California. One of the taxi operations was Yellow Cab of Los Angeles, which operated twelve hundred cabs, making it the third largest in the country. The original operation, Yellow Cab of San Francisco, had 503 licenses.

Fortunately, Rothschild did not live to see his taxi empire crumble. In 1962 the Westgate Corporation purchased Yellow Cab of California for $5.5 million. It did not, however, maintain Rothschild's concern for quality service. Westgate went bankrupt in 1976 owing $7.5 million in claims and $1 million in pensions. The individual taxi firms were once again separated; Yellow Cab of San Francisco was purchased by a group of 185 drivers.

### FRANK SAWYER

Frank Sawyer grew up in the West End of Boston, across the street from a livery stable. His education in the taxicab business began as he watched drivers rent horses and carriages for two dollars per day from the livery stable owner. By his early teens he was driving a taxi. The union scale was twenty-five cents an hour, and the Renaults and Franklins that he drove had no windshields or side windows. They had kerosene side lamps (he carried a can of kerosene with him), Presto headlamps, and spare tubes for flat tires.

In 1921 he started Checker Taxi Company with twelve cabs purchased from Yellow Cab Manufacturing and four Fords with planetary transmissions. The Fords did not last very long. Later, he bought some cabs from Checker Motors, an occasion which, according to Sawyer, resulted in Hertz's not letting him into the National Association of Taxicab Owners.[10] When he eventually bought more Yellows, he got in; in 1953 he was its president.

When Sawyer started in the business, cabs were used mainly by the wealthy; for the poor, they were a luxury saved for weddings, funerals, christenings, and bringing home the neighborhood "drunk." He soon recognized that proper behavior and dress by the drivers, as well as public recognition and approval of the firm's operation, were of vital importance. Working hard on his public image, he employed the slogan, "Don't take a chance; take a Checker" and advertised that if a young lady became unhappy with her date, she could go home in a Checker at no charge. The theory was that her parents would be so pleased at her safe return that they would pay.

Sawyer obtained an exclusive right to the cab stand at the Copley Plaza Hotel. That stand was so successful that he soon obtained similar rights at most of the best hotels, as well as at the docks and railroad stations. These stands not only nearly finished off the competition but they also had a profound effect on Sawyer's career. He began to buy valuable real estate for the cab stands and then more for the public parking lots. More important, in dealing with hotel owners, railroads, and shipping lines, he associated with the wealthiest people in the city, who were in a position to do him favors. Eventually, he obtained a virtual monopoly of the taxi business in Boston. However, the system of private taxicab stands did not survive the end of World War II.

During later years, Sawyer broadened his business interests. He started a mutual insurance company to insure his own cabs. As competing insurance firms went bankrupt during the Depression, taxi operators rushed to obtain insurance from Sawyer's company. To control the number of applicants, and to avoid being swamped with claims, he required that all applicants for insurance apply in person. He then moved the insurance office to Nantucket Island, which had no air service and very little boat service! In 1956 he purchased the Avis Rent-a-Car System from Richard S. Robie, who, until 1954, had been the operator of fifty-four Hertz locations in the Northeast. In 1962, Sawyer sold Avis to Lazard Freres, but retained the Boston Avis franchise for himself until he sold it in 1981. He still operates Checker Cab, Town Cab, Red Cab, Airport Limousine, and Copley Tours.

## A FAMILY BUSINESS

The growth of the taxi fleets in the first half of this century was the result of several factors. The technological and service innovations that occurred during these years were important, as was the leadership of those individuals who personally devoted themselves to the development of their businesses. These early taxicab pioneers eventually retired, however, leaving their businesses to others to operate. If it was the leadership of these early pioneers which built the industry, it was the manner in which that leadership was transferred which enabled some fleets to survive. The continued success of taxicab fleets soon became linked with a new factor: a family business orientation.

This has been evident even in the largest taxicab operation, the fleets related to Checker Motors. When Morris Markin took over ownership of taxicab companies in Chicago, New York, Minneapolis, and Pittsburgh, he quickly delegated the management of those operations to others, who in many instances later passed those management responsibilities on to their sons. Thus, the Markin taxicab operations became not only a Markin family business but also a business involving several other families.

Perhaps it was the involvement of these other families which enabled Markin to delegate so much authority to his managers. He insisted upon all of his operations following identical systems of maintenance, depreciation, accounting, and, most important of all, investigation and settlement of claims, which they insured through their own insurance firms. Detailed operating statements were regularly dispatched to Checker headquarters in Kalamazoo, and these reports were studied to compare the various operations with each other and with themselves over time. Markin limited his operating activities to the study of the statements being received in Kalamazoo, although he certainly did not spend all of his time in the Kalamazoo headquarters. In fact, Markin maintained an office at the headquarters of the New York operation even after he had moved his home to Kalamazoo. The Pittsburgh and Minneapolis operations, however, received little of Markin's direct attention. A good-humored joke among his managers was to guess the number of times that Markin had actually visited those two cities; no one guessed a number over a dozen.

In Chicago, Markin had two taxi operations for which he needed management executives. When Charles Gray, the first post-Hertz president of Yellow Cab Company, died suddenly in 1928, Markin selected Thomas B. Hogan to oversee the daily operations of the firm. Hogan had spent many years in the garage operations of Yellow and was well qualified to deal with the drivers and mechanics of the world's largest taxi fleet. To be president of Chicago Yellow Cab Company, the holding company which owned Yellow Cab Company, and its companion insurance company, Markin chose Benjamin Samuels who was a graduate of the University of Chicago and Harvard Law School and who had previously been handling litigation for Hertz. This arrangement continued until the deaths of both Hogan and Samuels. At Checker Taxi, Markin selected Michael Sokoll as chief executive officer. Sokoll had long handled the insurance and claims for Checker, even when it had been an association of owner-operators before Markin owned it. He was recognized as a meticulous operator with detailed insight into every aspect of the company's operations, and he supplemented that experience with a close, almost day-to-day relationship with Ralph Oakland, Checker Motor Company's accounting expert.

The two operating heads of Markin's Chicago operations, Sokoll and Samuels, could hardly have been more different. One was self-educated and self-informed concerning operations; the other was highly educated and sensitive to legal positions, public concerns, employee relations, and politics. Yet for a quarter of a century they led the taxicab industry of Chicago through a maze of major problems and conflicts. Indeed, their mutual respect and concerns, together with their similarity of views concerning the future of the taxicab industry, might well have posed a problem under the antitrust laws. Sokoll and Samuels faced all of the operating difficulties consequent to World War II: shortages of fuel, tires, vehicles, parts, and drivers; the unlicensed "veteran cabs" at the close of the war; and the flood of litigation with both the federal government and the city of Chicago. These two operators were always convinced that the ultimate end of this turmoil would be the survival of solvent and properly operated taxicab fleets. Their aspirations having been fulfilled, both died before the arrival of the next major innovation in the industry: the use of computers.

Succeeding Sokoll and Samuels were two "family" members. The management of Checker Taxi was taken over by Jerry E. Feldman, Markin's son-in-law, and Chicago Yellow's management was passed on to Samuels's son, Robert E. Samuels. These two brought into the industry the use of computers to handle the many operational details of providing taxicab service.

The family orientation has also been evident at Checker's two other operations. Yellow Taxi Company of Minneapolis, first operated by Claude Masters, was then managed by Jack Daley, Sr., later by Jack Daley, Jr., and then by Markin's grandson, Jeffrey Feldman. The Yellow Cab Company of Pittsburgh, operated for a period by the previous owners, was then managed by James P. Sinnott, the son of Carroll J. Sinnott, who had run the National Transportation Company, Markin's operation in New York City. So it was that Markin's entire taxicab holdings, plus three insurance companies and his airport bus operations, survived under "family" employees.

The same family orientation has been common in many other fleets throughout the country. In Columbus, Ohio, a fleet started by Max Glassman and Frank Kaufman was later passed on to their sons Marvin Glassman and Kenneth Kaufman. Yellow Cab Company in New Orleans was begun by George and Frank Toye and later operated by George Toye, Jr. Bell Cab Company in New York City was passed from Nat Levine to his son-in-law Ron Stoppelmann. Charlie's Taxi and Tours in Honolulu was developed by Charles Murita and later operated by his daughter, Dale S. Evans. The list goes on; in many cities those fleets that survived were those that were retained as family operations.

By contrast, one major taxicab operation which did not survive was also one which did not enjoy this family orientation. Yellow Cab Company of California, which owned most of the larger taxicab fleets on the West Coast, plus sightseeing bus operations and one airline, could not be passed on by its principal owner, W. Lansing Rothschild, to members of his family. When Rothschild became ill, he sold the company to C. Arnholt Smith. Fortunately, Rothschild did not live to see his enterprise disintegrate when Smith's Westgate Corporation later went bankrupt.

## THE LEGACY OF THE FLEETS

Throughout the country, in large cities and small, individual entrepreneurs were building local taxi fleets. The four cases discussed here illustrate this process, but they are by no means the only important examples. Still, they were among the first—particularly the first three discussed—and they exerted an influence over how taxi fleets were organized and managed in other cities.

The emergence of large fleets was a new phenomenon. With them came a temporary stabilization of local taxi industries, as well as the implementation of technological and operational advances. Traffic signals in Chicago, the dispatch telephone, new vehicles, and many other innovations were developed and tested by the owners of the large fleets of the 1920s.

The fleet operators were also responsible for starting the first national taxicab association. After preliminary meetings in 1917 and 1918, a small group of taxicab operators in 1919 formed the National Association of Taxicab Owners (NATO). This organization represented the taxi owners on a few legislative issues and served as a forum for sharing ideas and experiences. In 1938 these same operators formed the Cab Research Bureau in Cleveland; four years later NATO and the bureau became affiliated, a partnership which lasted until the mid-1960s. A second national organization, the American Taxicab Association (ATA), was formed in 1943 to represent smaller taxi firms. In 1966 the NATO and the ATA merged to form the International Taxicab Association.

In retrospect, the success of the fleet operators serves as a reminder of how different business conditions were in the 1920s. Absent were federal transit subsidies, minimum wage requirements, and a host of federal and state regulations, taxes, and restrictions. The fleet operators entered an industry which was technologically unsophisticated at a time when an individual's hard work and shrewdness determined, to a large measure, success or failure. Hertz, Markin, and many other individuals with meager educational and economic backgrounds were born in an era of opportunity.

Perhaps the most significant legacy of the early fleet owners was the conception of the taxi as a quality service for everyone and of the taxi driver as a respected professional. Reducing taxi fares, cleaning vehicles daily, and assuring neat, uniformed drivers were important service advances. Simultaneously, profit sharing, commissions, and fringe benefits were evidence of enlightened labor practices that were much ahead of their time. Unfortunately for the taxi industry, the movement toward such progressive practices would soon by stymied. Ahead lay the Depression and World War II, both of which were to change the image of the taxicab industry.

*Benjamin Samuels (1880–1963), chairman of Chicago Yellow Cab Company, Inc. (Collection of the author.)*

# 5

# THE DEPRESSION AND REGULATION

## ECONOMIC TURMOIL AND PUBLIC INTERVENTION

The stock market crash in late 1929 marked the onslaught of a depression which was to dominate the next ten years. The 1930s were much different from the previous fifteen years. The unemployment rate, which had steadily fallen to a low of 1.8 percent in 1926, had soared to 25.2 percent only seven years later. For nonfarm workers, the situation was even worse; a 2.9 percent unemployment rate in 1926 had become a 37.6 percent rate by 1933. Real income declined by 2.2 percent from 1930 to 1935 for persons lucky enough to find jobs; including unemployed persons the decline was a staggering 19.5 percent. Even the process of urbanization was brought to a virtual halt; the percentage of persons living in urban areas increased from 56.0 percent in 1930 to only 56.3 percent in 1940. Bounded by periods of affluence and wartime inflation, the Depression formed the bottom of a roller-coaster economic cycle.

The Depression had a profound effect on transportation. Intercity freight movements decreased, compounding the problems already faced by the railroads and leading to the Emergency Transportation Act of 1933. Trucking firms, on the other hand, increased in number, as unemployed persons rented or purchased secondhand trucks and entered the trucking industry. The ensuing intense competition resulted in rate wars and in a greater share of the freight market going to trucks at the expense of railroads. However, competition among trucking firms became so furious that the federal government had to act again, this time pushing through the Motor Carrier Act of 1935. Modeled after the existing railroad regulations, the Motor Carrier Act extended federal control over entry, routes, and rates to both the motor truck and intercity bus industries. Three years later the Civil Aeronautics Act of 1938 brought the airline industry under federal regulation. By the end of the Depression federal control pervaded every mode of interstate transportation.

One should not infer, however, that federal regulation was brought about entirely by the Depression or that without the Depression such federal control would never have happened. Probably federal legislation to control interstate transportation carriers would have happened regardless of the Depression. Yet, like the period of intense competition and industry instability that gave rise to railroad regulation in 1887, the Depression dramatically extended governmental concern over the reliability and stability of unregulated interstate carriers. The federal policy of responding to economic turmoil with regulation had been set in the late 1800s in the case of railroads and was uniformly extended to other interstate carriers in the 1930s.

The pattern of public intervention and control for urban transportation had also been established well before the Depression, but that industry was not an interstate one, and it was therefore the local and state governments that did the regulating. The problem that had attracted public concern was the product of the economic instability that followed the close of World War I.

Before the war, the streetcar had been financially healthy and unchallenged as an urban transportation carrier. In 1912, 93 percent of all mass transit riders were served by streetcars. The automobile was still a luxury, and the bus still an experiment. Streetcar companies enjoyed long-term municipal franchises which fixed the fares, usually at five cents. However, wartime inflation meant higher operating costs, and the ensuing economic troubles brought bankruptcy for one-third of the streetcar firms by 1918.[1]

At the close of the war the appearance of a new competitor, the jitney, exacerbated the financial problems of the streetcar. So named because of its five-cent fare, the jitney was a privately owned and operated automobile. It was neither a taxicab nor a bus; rather it was a vehicle which traveled the streetcar routes ahead of the streetcars and picked up persons awaiting streetcars. In 1916 about twenty-four thousand jitneys were in operation.[2]

The streetcar industry immediately felt the effects of the jitneys. In

Bridgeport, Connecticut, for example, it was estimated that in 1918 56 percent of the public transit passengers were carried by jitneys.[3] The streetcar industry responded by pushing for municipal antijitney laws. These laws and the relative inexperience of jitney operators in business matters combined to wipe out nearly all the jitneys by 1920. The antijitney laws, which, among other provisions, prohibited shared-riding, provided a lasting legal legacy of the jitneys. President Wilson also responded to the problems of the streetcar industry by commissioning a major study of the industry in 1919. While providing a valuable, in-depth analysis of the problems facing the streetcars, this study led to no federal programs or legislation regarding urban transit.[4]

Thus, when the economic turmoil of the Depression brought chaos in the taxicab industry, it was natural that local and state governments would respond with regulation. However, the problems that the industry faced in these years were not restricted to the taxicab; urban transportation in general was going through a difficult time.

## MASS TRANSIT IN TRANSITION

Two important changes were taking place in mass transit during the late 1920s and the Depression. One of these, which has received much attention from transit historians, was the replacement of the streetcar by the bus. This change, however, was only a part of a more important shift which has received comparably little attention: the replacement of transit with the automobile.

It is, of course, well known that the number of automobiles expanded rapidly during the 1910–30 period. In fact, over fifty times as many automobiles were registered in 1930 as in 1910. But, the effect of this increase can best be seen by examining the number of vehicles per driving-age person. In 1910 there were 0.007 vehicles per person in the 15–74 age group. Ten years later this ratio had risen to 0.130, and by 1930 it had further increased to 0.313. Successive decades found the ratio increasing much more slowly, meaning that the "automobilization" of the country occurred in the 1910–30 period rather than after World War II.

Unlike the jitneys, the automobile could not be made illegal by streetcar-sponsored laws. The streetcar, as well as the entire transit industry, began losing passengers to the automobile long before the Depression. These losses are evident both on a per capita basis and on an absolute basis. After holding constant during the 1910–20 decade, the number of annual transit rides per urban resident fell by over 20 percent during the succeeding two decades. Not only was transit not maintaining its share of the urban travel market after 1920, but it was also declining in absolute terms after ridership peaked in 1926. This decline was to be a long one; interrupted only by the abnormal conditions during World War II, it lasted until 1972.

Amid this general decline in the use of mass transit the streetcar did not fare well. In fact, while transit ridership was waning during the 1920s and 1930s, streetcar ridership was decreasing even faster. Total mileage of streetcar tracks peaked in 1916, and streetcar ridership began dropping after 1923. The cause of this shift was a relative of the automobile: the motor bus.

The bus was not exactly a new threat; it had come to the United States from England in 1905. The early buses, however, were noisy, expensive, and unreliable. Moreover, the public utilities, which owned many streetcar lines, were not eager to change to nonelectric vehicles. Not until 1925 did the bus emerge as a serious competitor to the streetcar. In that year the bus carried 9 percent of the mass transit passengers, compared with 77 percent for the streetcar.[5] A decade later those figures had changed to 21 percent and 60 percent, respectively. The bus was becoming more important as the streetcar was declining.

The streetcar industry did not accept its demise without a struggle. In 1929 presidents from twenty-five of the largest streetcar companies formed the Electric Railway Presidents' Conference. Collectively, they agreed to fund the development of a new, cheaper, faster, and more comfortable streetcar. Five years later and after having spent over one million dollars, they succeeded. In 1934 the Presidents' Conference Committee (PCC) Streetcar was unveiled. Fittingly, the PCC car was available just in time for Frank Sprague, the father of the original streetcar, to ride it a few weeks before his death in 1934. Nearly five thousand PCC cars were built, of which about eleven hundred were still in use in the late 1970s, and it proved to be an engineering masterpiece. However, the PCC arrived too late to reverse the decline of the streetcar industry.

The Depression years proved disastrous for the streetcar industry. Ridership plummeted by over 30 percent between 1930 and 1935 and by nearly 20 percent more during the following five years. In addition the industry lost a major source of its capital. The Public Utilities Holding Act of 1935 required electric power utility holding companies to divest themselves of such ancillary industries as the streetcar industry, and, with few exceptions, streetcar systems were put up for sale. Just when the streetcars most needed repair and replacement, their primary source of capital—the holding companies—was withdrawn. By 1940 only 45 percent of transit passengers were served by streetcars.

## THE TAXICAB INDUSTRY ON THE EVE OF THE DEPRESSION

Against the pattern of changes occurring in the mass transit industry in the 1920s, the taxicab industry was seemingly stable. Fleet operations were expanding, and public regulation of the industry was minimal. The 1920s were a period of rapid growth and economic prosperity for the industry. It was not, however, a completely tranquil period, as isolated taxicab "wars" broke out in several cities during the mid-1920s. These wars were a harbinger of the chaos that was to come during the Depression.

Before 1915 only a few local ordinances and very few state statutes regulated taxicabs; these were concerned with only a few topics, such as bonds of indemnity for damages and the posting of rates of fare. For example, Chicago required bonds in 1866 and the posting of fares as early as 1873. Interestingly, the bonds of indemnity protected the city, not injured passengers, who were not protected by law until compulsory insurance in the 1920s.

As the taxi industry expanded during the early 1920s, interest in more comprehensive municipal taxi regulation also increased. Until the Depression, however, there was not much concern with the limitation of numbers of licensed taxicabs. The industry was expanding at a rapid pace, spurred both by the rapid growth of the cities and by an even more rapid growth in the numbers of persons who were able to hire taxis and who wanted to take advantage of their newfound mobility. Thus, rather than limit the supply of taxis, municipal regulation focused on protecting passengers by limiting fares and requiring insurance. The insurance requirements seem to have been initiated by state governments and later adopted into city codes. One of the earliest such statutes was the 1921 Motor Vehicle Law in Illinois, which required ten-thousand-dollar minimum insurance but was found unconstitutional because of the high amount! By 1932 fourteen states had passed mandatory insurance laws. In addition, thirty cities not located in these fourteen states had enacted similar requirements.[6]

Without controls over entry into the industry, ruinous competition was possible and did occur in a few instances. Prior to 1937 New York City had no restrictions on entry; anyone wishing to own or drive a taxi could do so. In the summer of 1924, several firms cut the taxi rates from fifty cents to twenty-five cents per mile. According to Vidich, this action was based on the desire of automobile manufacturers to sell their cars.[7] These manufacturers either controlled New York taxi firms or were owed money by them. To sell more cars the manufacturers directed their taxi firms to lower fares, hoping to drive the other taxi firms out of business. The result was a rate war. Taxi fares dropped to ten cents per half mile making them comparable to the five-cent fare on the subway. Taxi ridership soared by 30 percent. Unfortunately, so did illegal activity. Cheating, hustling, false advertising, stealing, and extortion became common. At the insistence of the police commissioner, the taxi industry was placed under police control in 1925. That action ended the war, as unlicensed drivers were eliminated from the industry and taxi fares were stabilized at forty cents per mile.

Similar taxicab wars occurred in other cities during the 1920s. In Chicago, for instance, Checker and Yellow fought for supremacy in the fall of 1928, and one Checker driver was killed. One year later, in September 1929, the Chicago City Council passed a taxi ordinance which, for the first time, limited the number of taxicabs.

While the taxicab wars were scattered and brief, they played an important role in degrading the public image of the industry. During a time of Prohibition and gangsterism, the taxi wars increased the public awareness of illegal activities within the industry, regardless of how minor such activities were. The efforts of Hertz and others to promote the taxi driver as a dependable professional had been severely undercut.

## THE DEPRESSION: CHAOS AND REGULATION

Two factors made the taxicab industry particularly vulnerable to the economic convulsions of the Depression. First, in most cities the taxicab industry had no entry controls, meaning that there were no limits on the number of taxicabs. While many cities required a driver's permit, such permits were routinely given. Second, the taxicab industry was primarily a cash business, a fact which encouraged inexperienced operators to neglect depreciation costs and good maintenance practices. Together, these factors kept the taxi industry in a state of constant flux; new operators were continually entering and then soon leaving when they were unable to repair or replace their vehicles.

The Depression of the 1930s exacerbated this tendency. Soaring unemployment pushed countless persons onto the streets as taxi drivers. According to one estimate the United States in 1932 had 150,000 taxis, of which only 84,000 belonged to pre-Depression operators.[8] In New York City the number of cabs exploded to 30,000 in 1930.[9]

The expansion of the supply of taxi service at a time of economic depression meant that more taxis competed for fewer passengers. Rate wars flared in cities throughout the country. Rates, which had ranged between forty cents and seventy cents for the first mile, were cut by the new cab operators to fifteen cents and later to ten cents. In some cities, such as Washington, the cut-rate taxis actually were free, and many cities had "nickel" cabs, which charged five cents for any trip in the city.

These below-cost fares and the tremendous increase in numbers of taxis were disastrous for the industry. Taxi drivers were forced to rely on cheating, counterfeiting, and demanding tips in order to make any money. Legitimate taxicab operators went into bankruptcy, taking casualty insurers with them. Injured passengers and pedestrians went without compensation. The public outcry for regulation was nationwide.

The driving force behind the expansion in taxicab numbers was the automobile industry. With sales sagging, automobile manufacturers saw the taxicab industry as a place to unload new cars. A manufacturer would "sell" cars to a taxi operator on favorable financing terms with low down payments. The cut-rate taxi operator would then lease the cars as taxis to drivers for three to four dollars per day. The drivers had to recoup these lease fees by hustling business legitmately or by some illegitimate means. One contemporary estimate placed the average daily income of a taxi driver in Washington, D.C., at fifty-six cents.[10]

While the driver was put in a difficult competitive position, the manufacturer and the operator had a great deal. The manufacturer sold otherwise unsellable cars, and the operator received a guaranteed daily income with no risk. In fact, the manufacturer would urge an operator to purchase more cars by pointing out that the more cars leased, the more the operator's income. Liability for accidents was transferred to the driver by changing the lease agreements to long-term "purchase" agreements, thus making the driver entirely responsible for any damages. Such damages were by no means inconsequential, as accident rates for taxis skyrocketed.[11]

Taxi service on the streets was in a state of chaos. Cabs of every make were in service in most cities. The nonspecialized vehicles were quickly deteriorating, and their owners had little money to repair them. Fare gouging, cheating, and counterfeiting were common, and taxis clogged the streets of large cities. One observer at the time made a careful study of the problem and concluded:

> The taxicab industry is in a thoroughly unhealthy condition.
> In many of the largest cities of the country it is almost entirely in the hands of irresponsible operators, utterly unqualified to carry on an organized transportation enterprise. Financial responsibility is almost totally lacking. Ability to assume full liability for accidents is an exception rather than the rule. . . .
>
> These difficulties have largely been brought about by the invasion of the legitimate taxicab field by financially irrespon-

*A 1935 model taxi manufactured by Checker Motors Corporation shown in front of Chicago City Hall. Examining the taxi are Thomas B. Hogan, president of Yellow Cab Company; Morris Markin, president of Checker Motors Corporation; Mayor Edward J. Kelly; and Benjamin Samuels, president of Chicago Yellow Cab Company, Inc. (Collection of the author.)*

*A Checker-built cab of the late 1930s. The retractable rear roof caused numerous problems, and this option was only offered one year. (Collection of the author.)*

sible operators of light, cheap passenger automobiles masquerading as "taxicabs."[12]

Newspapers throughout the country called for the regulation of taxicabs. The *Cincinnati Enquirer* for 22 September 1932 said: "Taxicabs are a public service and should be regulated as such." On 22 February 1933 the *New York Times* stated: "The industry cries aloud for regulation.... Too many cabs on the street,... operators... without financial responsibility,... many avoidable accidents,... these are but a few of the evils to be remedied." Other papers repeated these charges against the chaos of nonregulation.

In his analysis of the problem, Simpson reached the same conclusion: "As the full effects of the wave of cut-rate driver-rental operation ... become recognized, it may be expected that regulation ... will be widely adopted, because of the obvious advantages of discouraging unorganized and irresponsible operation of public vehicles."[13]

The old-line taxi operators also supported regulation. At its 1930 annual meeting NATO passed a resolution that contained the following five provisions:

1. Place taxicabs under control of a state or city utility commission.

2. Require public convenience and necessity to be met before licensing additional cabs.

3. Require operators to demonstrate financial responsibility for damages.

4. Require taximeters.

5. Designate maximum and minimum rates for fares.[14]

The regulation movement spread throughout the country. In Massachusetts, Frank Sawyer urged the state to regulate taxis, and in 1930 the legislature limited the number of cabs in Boston to 1,525 (the same as in 1980). New York City first limited the number of cabs in 1932 under the sponsorship of Mayor Jimmy Walker, but when Walker was forced to resign when it was discovered that he had been bribed by one of the taxi companies, the attempt at regulation failed.

Five years later, however, the Haas Act in New York City froze the number of taxi medallions at 13,500.[15] In Chicago a 1934 ordinance restricted the number of taxis to 4,108, a number which was lowered to 3,000 in 1937. Baltimore taxis were placed under state regulations beginning in 1931.

Soon taxicab regulation was commonplace. In April 1932, Simpson surveyed states and cities over 25,000 population to determine the extent of taxi regulation. Simpson found that 35 percent of the cities over 100,000 and 19 percent of the cities between 25,000 and 100,000 had regulations that made taxis public utilities and subject to the securing of certificates of public convenience and necessity.[16] In some of these cities the requirements for certificates were actually state requirements; eight states had such a requirement. At least two other cities had fixed ceilings on the number of permits. At least 53 cities over 25,000 population required taximeters, and 22 cities (out of 125 for which ordinances were examined) set the rates a taxi operator could charge. Specially built taxi vehicles were required in seven cities, while eight others specified design features that a taxi vehicle had to meet.

This trend toward regulation became more prevalent as the Depression wore on. The taxicab industry, which as late as 1929 had been almost totally unregulated, had in a few years become the subject of much public regulation, and this regulation was surprisingly uniform throughout the United States. It centered on five major areas:

1. *Entry controls.* These generally were along the lines of those regulating other transportation facilities: the number of licenses was to be that which was required by the public convenience and necessity and subject to a priority in which those already holding licenses could apply for any additional licenses.

2. *Fixed rates of fare.* Like those of other regulated transportation facilities, fares for taxis were to be set at an amount that would guarantee a reasonable rate of return on invested capital.

3. *Financial responsibility.* By insurance (carried in solvent and responsible insurance companies) or by cash reserves, there

had to be assurances to the public that any claims for injuries sustained would be paid. In addition, the licensee had to have sufficient funds to keep his equipment in good condition and repair and to replace it when it became worn out.

4. *Condition of vehicles*. The public was to be assured that it would be carried safely through inspection programs.

5. *Assurance of service*. Regulations encouraged the organization of fleets of taxicabs, thereby assuring the public better transportation service through the ability of large companies to maintain dispatching facilities and stands.

These concepts were very acceptable to the taxicab operators, and they were quick to invest in vehicles and facilities. The public, too, responded well to a better-regulated industry, and the use of taxi services expanded rapidly. Those charged with regulating taxicabs found that an industry made up more and more of large fleets allowed for practical and efficient regulation.

## A TRANSFORMED INDUSTRY

The end of the Depression found the taxicab industry fundamentally changed. No longer was it a robust, expanding, unregulated industry with a positive public image. The industry had been stabilized and, like virtually all other commercial transportation modes, had become categorized as a public utility. Other more subtle changes had also occurred. Most attempts at building multicity taxi empires had failed, leaving the taxi industry one in which companies were primarily locally owned—and regulated. Despite Hertz's attempts—which are not clearly documented—he was not able to maintain ownership of taxi operations in more than one city. Markin did achieve multicity operations, and the West Coast firm started by Rothschild was also successful in this regard. With few other exceptions, the remaining taxicabs were owned and operated by local entrepreneurs. No federal taxi laws were enacted, and only a few states passed any form of taxi regulation. The remaining regulations were all enacted locally.

Taxi regulations of the 1930s also brought the increased use of taximeters and ended zone and flat fares in many areas. While it had the salutary effect of making the passenger feel that the fare was computed honestly—not always an accurate feeling—the taximeter requirement made the taxi operators providers of exclusive-ride service. Unable to provide shared-ride service, taxis could no longer compete with mass transit modes. This was welcomed by the mass transit operators, who had lost a great deal of revenue to the cut-rate taxis in the early 1930s.

Perhaps the most troublesome holdover from this period, however, was the negative image that the industry and its drivers had with the public. Hertz and other early operators had treated drivers as respected professionals and had worked to promote that image among the public. The taxi rate wars and the accompanying hustling and cheating by the drivers to make a living during the 1930s had changed all that. Unfortunately for the industry—and the public—the taxi driver had become an individual who was distrusted by both the public and the owners.

It is interesting to consider what the industry might have become had the Depression and the taxi rate wars not occurred. It is likely that regulation would have come eventually, although not as a response to crisis. Perhaps in a less heated atmosphere regulations could have been designed that would have allowed for innovation. Drivers might not have gained such a negative image, and taxis would now be regulated by the officials who license bus drivers rather than by police officers. In short, the industry might have evolved in a much different way.

# 6

## WAR AND RECOVERY

World War II occurred as the United States was trying to overcome the ravages of the Depression. The productive capacities of factories, which had been vastly underutilized during the Depression, were suddenly taxed to the limit. Unemployment, rampant during the Depression, practically vanished; by 1940 unemployment had only declined to 14.6 percent, but just three years later it was 1.9 percent. Factories that had once produced civilian consumer items were switched to war production, and materials such as rubber and gasoline were rationed for the civilian consumer. Real income during the war years also increased; between 1940 and 1943 real income grew by 57.8 percent.

The effect of these changes on the urban transit industry was dramatic. Transit ridership, which had peaked in 1926, had fallen by 21.5 percent from 1930 to 1935.[1] By 1940, it had risen by only 7 percent over the 1935 level, and streetcars had continued to decrease in importance to the point that only 45 percent of transit passengers were served by them. Overall, the transit industry was experiencing over-capacity and economic decline.

The war reversed those conditions. Factories switched to twenty-four hour shifts and six-day weeks. High employment in a time of gas rationing sent people back to the urban transit systems. From 1940 to 1943 ridership grew by 168 percent, even though employment within the transit industry grew by less than 20 percent. Nighttime, or "owl," transit service burgeoned to accommodate the increase in night-shift workers. In some cities six-day work weeks and Saturday shopping combined to make that traditional off day the peak day for transit ridership. Equipment and employees were hard-pressed to serve this soaring demand for transit rides. New transit vehicles were available until 1942; but from 1942 through 1945 the number of buses increased by only 8 percent.

After years of decline in the industry the transit boom during the war must have looked like a good omen to transit operators. No new bankruptcies occurred during 1940–45, and the transit firms—which were still privately owned—were beginning to pay off long-standing debts with their new profits. One observer at the time recognized the abnormal conditions of the war and the threat of the automobile, but predicted that wartime ridership gains would not all be lost after the war.[2] The future for transit firms looked bright as they entered the postwar years with reduced debts and increased riderships.

## TAXICABS DURING THE WAR

The taxicab industry was shrinking when the war broke out. From 1939 to 1940 the number of taxicabs in the 391 largest United States cities fell from 43,032 to 37,841, a drop of 12 percent.[3] For the country as a whole, the size of the industry was about 65,000 cabs, according to one estimate for 1940.[4] Another source estimated the number of cabs one year later to be 55,400.[5] The supply of taxis, however, is better measured by the number of persons per cab. In 1940, for the 91 largest cities, the ratio was 1,165 persons per cab; excluding New York and Chicago, the ratio was 1,500 persons per cab. Moreover, while Washington had a cab for every 200 persons, Pittsburgh had to make do with one for every 2,661 persons.[6]

One of the first effects of the war was the suspension of taxicab manufacturing, as the taxicab factories were switched to wartime production. No new cabs were produced during the five years after 1941. Checker Cab Manufacturing Company (later Checker Motors Corporation), the major producer, was particularly hard hit; it produced no taxicabs from 1941 to 1947. In the patriotic spirit of the time Checker sold its tooling for scrap metal to build weapons, so it had to retool at the conclusion of the war. During the war Checker built a variety of equipment for the army, including three jeeps.

The lack of new cabs created a great hardship for the cab industry.

Accustomed to replacing their vehicles every one or two years, taxi operators suddenly had to maintain old vehicles indefinitely. As a result, the number of taxicabs in the country declined from 55,400 in 1941 to 48,389 in 1945. By 1945 the nation's taxis were a sorry lot. It was estimated in that year that one-fourth of the cabs were in the repair shop on any given day. Repair costs were estimated to be fifteen hundred dollars per cab per year, an amount which was equal to the cost of a new taxi before the war.[7] Not only were no new vehicles available, but replacement parts were virtually nonexistent and mechanics were scarce. Compounding these woes, the streets were full of potholes because of the lack of wartime street maintenance.

Their inability to obtain specially built taxis was particularly hard on New York operators. New York City required all of its taxis to have the following characteristics: room for five passengers behind the driver and no passengers in the front seat; a trunk-mounted luggage rack; and a grill in the trunk to preclude the transporting of dead bodies. Only Checker, Desoto, and Packard had models that fulfilled these requirements for a "jumbo" cab. Thus New York taxi operators had even less flexibility than did operators in most other cities in using standard sedans when wartime taxi production ceased. New York finally allowed smaller cabs in July 1954.

While the supply of taxis dwindled, the demand for taxis soared. The largest jump in ridership occurred in 1942, when ridership increased by 33.2 percent. That same year the number of taxis decreased by the largest percentage for a one-year period, 8.3 percent. Table 6.1 shows that this pattern persisted during the war years: shrinking supply and increasing demand. Everywhere, soldiers on weekend leaves, factory workers, and others piled into taxis just as they climbed aboard transit vehicles. The rapidly deteriorating taxicab fleet strained under the pressure.

The pattern for taxicabs differed appreciably from that for the transit industry. Transit vehicles increased in numbers throughout the war years, as "mothballed" vehicles were pressed into service; the peak in number of vehicles occurred in 1947. Ridership increased dramatically in 1942 and only gradually thereafter, until it peaked in 1946. During the war years taxi operators faced increased ridership with a decreased number of vehicles; as will be discussed later, the

TABLE 6.1. *War and Postwar Taxicab Trends*

| Year | Taxicab Vehicles | Taxicab Passengers (millions) |
|---|---|---|
| 1941 | 55,400 | 967 |
| 1942 | 50,800 | 1,288 |
| 1943 | 48,464 | 1,446 |
| 1944 | 47,301 | 1,616 |
| 1945 | 48,389 | 1,650 |
| 1946 | 62,905 | 1,887 |
| 1947 | 73,473 | 1,808 |
| 1948 | 81,701 | 1,967 |
| 1949 | 79,741 | 1,749 |
| 1950 | 79,001 | 1,668 |
| 1951 | 78,764 | 1,578 |
| 1952 | 76,402 | 1,523 |
| 1953 | 78,082 | 1,489 |
| 1954 | 78,191 | 1,404 |

Source: Cab Research Bureau, *Taxicabs and Trends*.

immediate postwar years saw a sharp rise in both ridership and number of vehicles, peaking for both in 1948.

The taxi industry came under federal emergency regulation during the war. The Office of Defense Transportation (ODT) was empowered to control the operating characteristics of the nation's taxi fleets. Effective 1 September 1942 the ODT implemented the following taxicab regulations:

1. No new taxi vehicles could be built.
2. No cruising.
3. No use of taxis for recreation trips.
4. No use of taxis for deliveries.
5. No excessive speeds.

6. No taxi trips more than ten miles outside a city's limits.

7. No trips longer than thirty-five miles.

The ODT also controlled the amount of fuel and number of tires allocated to the taxi industry. Taxi operators received an S-type fuel rationing card, which entitled a taxi to enough gasoline to go about one hundred miles per day.

The ODT also had the power to alter the mileage that taxis were allowed to operate. In 1942 the ODT ordered Chicago taxi operators to restrict their 1943 mileage to the 1941 level or receive no more recapped tires, which was the only type of tires available to taxi firms. To comply, Chicago Yellow Cab limited drivers to 60 percent of the miles driven in 1942. In New York the number of taxis was reduced from 11,700 in March 1942 to 9,352 by December of that same year.

In January 1943 the ODT further required all taxi operators with more than ten cabs to submit contingency plans outlining how they would accommodate mileage cuts of 10 percent, 20 percent, and 30 percent. With the urging of the ODT, city after city introduced emergency changes in taxi regulations to aid the industry in its conservation efforts. In December 1943 the ODT praised the taxi industry for two achievements: by implementing shared-riding in forty-five cities, taxis had provided an estimated 250 million additional rides with no increase in mileage, and by coordinating dispatching and repair services between firms, the industry had saved an estimated 1.25 million gallons of fuel a year.

Both of these wartime efforts—shared-riding and local coordination—were successful despite the refusal of New York City to permit shared-riding. New York refused to permit shared-riding because of fear that women might be subjected to affronts by other taxi passengers. However, a survey of the forty-five participating cities showed that thirty-eight of them reported no such incidents in their cities.[8]

Although the war was a time of shortages for the taxi industry, it was also a time of economic prosperity. The ridership increases meant large revenue increases too. For the industry as a whole, revenues increased 138 percent between 1941 and 1945 and 251 percent between 1941 and 1948. Greater revenues and fewer taxis meant a bonanza for taxi drivers. Drivers who had received an average of eight to nine dollars per day in 1941 received more than eleven dollars per day one year later.[9] The following year, estimates placed the taxi driver's earnings at twice the prewar levels.[10] In New York City the income of taxi firms was estimated to be up by 60 percent in 1942 compared with 1941, and the Parmelee Company's financial statement for taxi service in its four cities during the first nine months of 1942 showed a profit of $596,693, compared with a deficit of $90,615 for a comparable period in 1941. For those operators who could find tires, fuel, drivers, and vehicles that would run, the war meant unprecedented profits.

## POSTWAR: VETERANS' CABS

The end of the war brought a rapid change in employment, production, and, of course, demand for transportation. Factories switched back to civilian production and eliminated extra shifts and weekend production. The number looking for work grew, as returning servicemen entered the labor force. In fact, unemployment rose from 1.2 percent in 1944 to 5.9 percent five years later. Transit ridership dropped in 1947, beginning a long-term decline that was not to be reversed until thirty years later.

At least in the short run, the taxi industry experienced a similar trend. New York operators cited a 10–20 percent drop in 1946. For the industry as a whole, however, ridership increased in 1946, dropped in 1947, and rose again to peak in 1948. During the four years from 1948 to 1952 the taxi industry experienced a 22.6 percent drop in ridership, while the transit industry as a whole experienced a decrease of 30.6 percent. Much of this drop was experienced by the streetcar industry, which declined in ridership by over 60 percent during those four years.

Unfortunately, supply and demand within the taxi industry were again out of synchronization. As demand was dropping rapidly, the supply of taxis was increasing. Table 6.1 shows that the number of licensed cabs actually was decreasing, but it does not show unlicensed cabs, which were increasing dramatically. These unlicensed cabs were known as "vet cabs."

To understand the vet-cab phenomenon one must keep in mind the postwar conditions within the taxi industry. Most cities limited the number of taxicabs and had ordinances specifying requirements for the licensing of drivers and the issuance of new permits. Although employers rehired employees who had worked for them—as they were required to do by law—a serious unemployment problem existed. Returning servicemen had also been given first priority on new automobiles produced. Finally, the taxi industry had been a highly profitable one during the preceding few years. For thousands of returning servicemen the course was obvious: buy a car and enter the taxi business. However, the limits on the numbers of taxis presented many cities with a dilemma: could they deny taxi licenses to persons who had just returned from fighting to protect their nation?

In city after city this dilemma was eventually solved, although not without a great deal of anguish. Exservicemen with converted automobiles and little or no insurance formed associations and companies and entered the the taxi business. In some cases they were granted licenses by city governments; in other cases they were not. The ones denied licenses often operated anyway; often they charged no fare to avoid the legal definition of a "taxicab," but made it clear that they expected tips. In a repetition of the situation of the early Depression years the taxi industry was again the victim of unemployment and economic crisis. Denying veterans a chance in private business was a political issue, and the situation was far too risky to induce many local officials to invoke the existing laws against exservicemen. The term *vet cab* became as common as *Yellow Cab*.

In Los Angeles at the end of the war 142 veterans paid two thousand dollars each to form the War Veterans Taxicab Association. However, the city had previously granted a franchise for taxicab service to Yellow Cab of Los Angeles. After operating "free" cabs and concentrating political support, the association persuaded the city to revoke the Yellow Cab franchise and grant its members licenses. Two years later the association experienced financial problems and was sold to Earl Muntz, a wealthy car dealer, who changed its name to Muntz Cab Company. The association had been losing thirty-nine thousand dollars per month and owed Union Oil Company over five hundred thousand dollars. No doubt one factor which contributed to the failure of the association was an oversupply of taxis on the streets. The number of cabs was 50 percent higher in 1946 than it had been before the war.[11]

A similar situation occurred in Chicago. The Chicago City Council had first limited the number of taxis in 1929. On 18 May 1934 the city passed its first franchise ordinance, which limited the number of taxis to 4,108. The Depression, however, continued to decrease taxi ridership; many independent operators were forced to give up, and Yellow and Checker incurred large losses. Drivers' wages were extremely low. Since the 1934 ordinance had granted franchises to Yellow and Checker, the city had no way to reduce the number of taxicab licenses other than by voluntary action. Proposing to the industry that it surrender sufficient licenses to bring the total down to 3,000, the city agreed that whenever additional licenses were issued, those who had surrendered licenses would be given first priority. With this agreement in 1937, independents surrendered 37 licenses and Yellow and Checker surrendered 1,071, of which 571 came from Yellow and 500 were from Checker. This entire procedure was carried out by ordinance in 1937 in accordance with the ordinance of 1934, which was later held by the Illinois Supreme Court to be an enforceable contract.

Thus, the returning exservicemen, with their petitions for taxi licenses, touched off a lengthy political and legal battle involving the veterans, the city, and Checker and Yellow. The veterans formed the American Cab Drivers Association for Discharged Veterans and petitioned the city for permits. In January 1946 Chicago granted them 250 permits, and Yellow Cab immediately filed suit against the city seeking an injunction against the issuance of these new permits based upon the 1937 agreement that promised Yellow and Checker any new permits up to the number surrendered by them. Yellow's petition was upheld by both the circuit court and the Illinois Supreme Court. The veterans responded by sending a caravan of 250 taxis to Washington to publicize their predicament. Mayor Edward Kelly urged the council to issue 275 special permits to the veterans, and, bowing to the political pressure, Yellow and Checker agreed not to oppose these new special permits. One month later, however, the council authorized 495 more special permits. After numerous legal battles, which included several procedural errors on the part of the city in conducting public hearings on the matter, Chicago issued 950 special permits for veterans in 1948. These permits were renewed annually thereafter. Surveys taken while the issue was still being argued showed that the number of unlicensed vehicles on the streets reached as many as 2,300 in 1947.

The federal government also responded to political pressures arising from the veterans' protests. In August 1946 it brought suit against Yellow Cab Company, Morris Markin, and virtually all the companies in the Parmelee group. The suit charged violations of both the Sherman Anti-Trust Act and the Clayton Act and claimed that the defendants had established vertically integrated monopolies. The suit was soon dismissed by the federal court, and the United States Supreme Court upheld that decision three years later, in the first Supreme Court decision holding that vertically integrated monopolies were not a violation of the Sherman and Clayton acts. More important for taxicab operators, it ruled that taxi operations were not engaged in interstate commerce and hence were insulated from federal jurisdiction, the Sherman and Clayton acts in particular. Later, the National Labor Relations Act expanded the definition of interstate commerce, and taxicab operations no longer enjoyed this legal immunity.

Many other cities experienced the problem of vet cabs. New York had sixteen hundred veterans apply for licenses in 1945 and 1946, and a few of these veterans were given licenses.[12] In San Francisco the Veterans' Taxicab Company received thirty-four of fifty new permits granted in August 1946, and in Pittsburgh, the Peoples Cab Company was given forty-two licenses. In Philadelphia the veterans were not so fortunate, as they were denied operating rights. In Washington, where no entry controls existed, the number of taxis in 1946 reached 9,107, almost double the 1940 level.[13] Driver earnings in Washington at the same time plummetted to about half of the levels enjoyed during the war.

In the cities faced with cab requests from veterans the price paid by everyone involved was severe. At a time when the country was changing from a wartime to a peacetime economy and the demand for taxi service was declining, the veterans' petitions for taxi licenses evoked a difficult, emotional controversy. For returning servicemen a taxi permit meant an entrepreneurial opportunity in an industry that they remembered from the war years to be a lucrative one, but which after the war was plagued by an oversupply of taxis. For the established taxi operators the veterans' petitions meant long and expensive legal battles at a time when they were trying to replace their worn-out vehicles and when taxi ridership was falling. For city officials it was a difficult political dilemma. In such a situation, there could be no winners, and the public image of the taxi industry dropped again.

## THE POSTWAR TAXI INDUSTRY

Despite the turmoil created by the vet cabs, the years immediately after World War II were a period of recovery for the taxi industry. As the automobile manufacturers gradually increased production, operators replaced worn-out taxis and expanded fleets. Table 6.1 shows that this expansion extended until 1948, after which the number of taxis declined.

By the end of 1947 there were about 80,000 taxicabs in the United States. A survey conducted by the International City Managers Association in October 1947 elicited responses from 836 cities over 10,000 population.[14] These cities reported a total of 64,985 taxicabs, or 855 persons per taxi. The availability of taxis varied with city size, however; the smallest cities (10,000–25,000) had the most taxis (704 persons per taxi) and the cities in the 100,000 to 250,000 category the fewest (1,176 persons per taxi). An analysis in 1947 of 360 taxicab ordinances revealed that 73 used the population-to-cab ratio as a means of limiting the number of taxis.[15] Most cities limited the number of taxicabs in some manner.

The postwar years saw the widespread adoption of the two-way radio. The radio had been introduced during the war, but not until after the war did it become common throughout the industry. In 1947 NATO and the ATA formed a joint committee to deal with the problems created by the proliferation of requests for radio frequencies within the industry.

Perhaps the major achievement of the industry in the postwar years

TABLE 6.2. *Distribution of Postwar Public Transportation Ridership*

| Year | Public Transportation Passengers (millions) | Percentage of Passengers by Mode | | | | |
|---|---|---|---|---|---|---|
| | | Taxicabs | Bus | Streetcar | Rapid Rail | Trolley Bus |
| 1946 | 21,006 | 9.0 | 41.0 | 32.2 | 12.8 | 5.0 |
| 1947 | 20,095 | 9.0 | 42.9 | 29.8 | 13.0 | 5.3 |
| 1948 | 19,279 | 10.2 | 46.1 | 24.6 | 12.8 | 6.3 |
| 1949 | 17,000 | 10.3 | 48.8 | 20.5 | 13.0 | 7.5 |
| 1950 | 15,513 | 10.8 | 49.5 | 18.0 | 13.6 | 8.1 |
| 1951 | 14,459 | 10.9 | 51.4 | 15.0 | 14.1 | 8.5 |
| 1952 | 13,549 | 11.2 | 52.6 | 12.7 | 14.6 | 8.9 |

Source: Cab Research Bureau, *Taxicabs and Trends*.

was that it was able to maintain its share of the public transportation market, a market which was declining in size. As shown in Table 6.2 the taxi's share of the market actually rose slightly from 1946 through 1952. This gain is illusory, however, since ridership for all modes of public transportation was declining. The streetcar was simply declining more rapidly than the other modes, meaning that the shares of a declining market were shifting.

The effects of the war—and postwar changes—can be seen in Table 6.3. The average number of miles driven per passenger carried fell during the war and then rose steeply during the postwar recovery. The decrease during the war is no doubt partially attributable to the increased sharing of taxis by passengers. After the war, as shared-riding declined and as more people moved to the suburbs, average trip lengths again rose. This increase was an important one for the taxi industry: less shared-riding and longer trip lengths meant more unpaid miles.

TABLE 6.3. *Taxicab Trip Length*

| Year | Taxicab Miles per Passenger |
|---|---|
| 1941 | 2.26 |
| 1942 | 1.99 |
| 1943 | 1.83 |
| 1944 | 1.98 |
| 1945 | 2.04 |
| 1946 | 2.28 |
| 1947 | 2.71 |
| 1948 | 2.65 |
| 1949 | 2.82 |
| 1950 | 3.00 |
| 1951 | 3.10 |
| 1952 | 3.16 |
| 1953 | 3.23 |
| 1954 | 3.38 |

Source: Cab Research Bureau, *Taxicabs and Trends*.

In many respects the taxi industry that emerged from the postwar years would change little over the next two decades. The regulatory structure had been revised to allow vet cabs, but remained essentially intact after that. DeSoto and Packard left the taxi manufacturing business to Checker, which in October 1955 introduced the Checker vehicle that, except for minor changes, was to be produced in the same model for two decades. The years 1950–70 were years of seeming stability, but pressures for change were at work. In the 1970s these pressures could not be ignored.

# 7

## FEDERAL INVOLVEMENT

For the taxicab industry, the decades of the 1960s and 1970s meant the emergence of a major new influence—the federal government. With the exception of the years during World War II, when the Office of Defense Transportation controlled taxi operations, the taxi industry had had very little interaction with the federal government. Radio frequencies were controlled by the Federal Communications Commission, and the Internal Revenue Service was certainly an influence on taxi operators. Beyond that, however, there was little federal interaction. Nor was the industry much influenced by state governments. Most government involvement with the taxi industry originated in local governments, which in most states were the agencies responsible for regulating taxis.

The 1960s and 1970s dramatically changed that situation. The Department of Transportation was created, as were comparable departments at the state level in many states. Other federal agencies set up a variety of local transportation programs which had profound effects for taxi operators. In the 1970s the scarcity of fuel brought the taxi industry into direct involvement with agencies responsible for the allocation of energy supplies. By the end of the 1970s the once rather isolated taxi industry had moved its association headquarters to Washington and was thoroughly involved with a variety of federal—and state—agencies.

The taxi industry was not unique in experiencing greater federal involvement; many other industries during the same period also felt this influence. The taxi industry was, however, unique in that the federal involvement was largely indirect: that is, few federal actions were explicitly focused on the taxi industry. Rather, most of the federal actions affecting taxi operators were aimed at urban transit systems and other competitors of the taxicab.

One important legal dimension to the growth of the federal involvement in the taxicab industry should be mentioned here. As discussed in the previous chapter, the Supreme Court had ruled in the Justice Department suit against Chicago Yellow Cab that the Sherman and Clayton acts did not apply to the taxi industry, because the defendants were not engaged in interstate commerce. For many years this ruling protected the taxi industry from federal regulation. The National Labor Relations Act, however, changed the legal framework for federal involvement, with respect to labor practices, at least, by bringing under federal jurisdiction all businesses that "affect commerce." By interpretation the term *affect commerce* came to include the purchase of materials (such as gasoline and vehicles) in interstate commerce. Thus, the National Labor Relations Board has jurisdiction over labor disputes within the taxicab industry. As shall be seen later, the involvement of the NLRB, like that of other federal agencies, was to have a profound affect on the industry.

## FEDERAL TRANSIT ASSISTANCE

Despite the optimism of Simpson and others that the World War II transit ridership boom would not entirely dissipate after the war, it did.[1] After peaking in 1946 at 23,372 million riders, urban transit ridership fell, reaching 17,246 million in 1950, a figure equivalent to the transit ridership peak reached in 1926.[2] Arguing that by 1950 any wartime effects should have disappeared, Smerk uses 1950 as a date with which to compare ridership levels and financial performance for the following two decades.[3] The resulting trends in ridership, income, and expense per passenger are shown in Table 7.1.

As the table shows, transit experienced a long and severe decline after 1950. By 1955 transit ridership had fallen by over 33 percent compared with 1950. In fact, the 1955 ridership was 11,529 million, almost exactly the low reached during the Depression year 1934. Thus, the decline in ridership, which had been slight before the war, accelerated dramatically after the war.

It is not surprising that this decline in ridership produced economic problems for the transit systems. Fare increases approximately offset

TABLE 7.1. *Transit Operating Trends*

| | Percent of Values for 1950 | | |
|---|---|---|---|
| Year | Ridership | Operating Income | Operating Expense per Passenger |
| 1950 | 100.00 | 100.00 | 100.0 |
| 1955 | 66.85 | 83.93 | 146.6 |
| 1960 | 54.47 | 46.24 | 182.6 |
| 1965 | 47.85 | −15.99 | 221.3 |
| 1970 | 42.51 | −434.25 | 344.0 |
| 1975 | 40.43 | −2566.67 | 676.0 |

Source: Smerk, *Urban Mass Transportation*, pp. 146–47; for 1975, American Public Transit Assocation, *Transit Factbook*.

the ridership declines during the 1950–70 period, meaning that total revenues remained nearly constant. However, as shown in Table 7.1, costs rose steeply. In 1963 the industry experienced a deficit, a financial condition from which it has never emerged.

The response of the transit industry to postwar losses in ridership was to cut costs. As shown in Table 7.2, the industry reduced employment levels, meaning that nondriver personnel was cut and fewer vehicles were operated. Transit systems curtailed service, as expressed in vehicle mileage per route-mile, a fact which appeared to transit users as less frequent service, and they also purchased fewer new vehicles (until the granting of federal aid in 1964).

One response to the financial troubles of the transit industry was for local governments to purchase the transit systems. Public ownership was rare as late as 1948, when only thirty-six transit systems were publicly owned.[4] As shown in Table 7.3, this situation changed dramatically. In 1975 publicly owned systems carried 90 percent of all transit passengers.[5]

While most publicly owned systems are owned by local governments, the money to purchase them came mostly from the federal government. Beginning in 1961, Congress established a small transit

TABLE 7.2. *Transit Service Trends*

| | Percent of Values for 1950 | | |
|---|---|---|---|
| Year | Employees | Vehicle Miles per Route-Mile | New Equipment |
| 1950 | 100.00 | 100.00 | 100.00 |
| 1955 | 82.50 | 83.53 | 79.63 |
| 1960 | 65.16 | 70.17 | 105.63 |
| 1965 | 60.41 | 60.56 | 117.37 |
| 1970 | 57.51 | 60.97 | 57.37 |
| 1975 | 66.58 | n.a. | 176.69 |

Source: Smerk, *Urban Mass Transportation*, p. 156; for 1975, American Public Transit Association, *Transit Factbook*.

TABLE 7.3. *Public Ownership of Transit*

| | Numbers of Transit Systems | |
|---|---|---|
| Year | Total | Publicly Owned |
| 1948 | 1,400 | 36 |
| 1959 | 1,225 | 52 |
| 1964 | 1,152 | 79 |
| 1967 | 1,138 | 98 |
| 1970 | 1,079 | 141 |
| 1975 | 947 | 333 |

Source: Mossman, *Principles*, p. 9; American Public Transit Association, *Transit Factbook*.

program, which included money only for loans and demonstrations. This program was certainly not adequate to meet the financial crisis facing transit systems. It provided only loans, not grants, and it failed to charge a specific federal agency with responsibility for transit problems. It was, however, a beginning.

Three years later the transit operators got the grant program they were seeking. The Urban Mass Transportation Act of 1964 inaugurated a much more ambitious federal transit program.[6] Successive congressional actions have amended and extended the 1964 act, but it remains the foundation of federal transit funding.

While funding under the 1964 act was modest—$375 million over three years—the act was of enormous importance for two reasons. First, it established a federal precedent for giving—not lending—money to fund transit operations. Second, it established the rules and procedures under which such grants would be given. The federal funds, which were to be used only for capital expenditures, could be given only to local public agencies, although public agencies could in turn use the funds to purchase buses for private firms. This restriction meant that Congress opted not to reinforce private ownership through a subsidy program but instead implicitly to encourage public takeover of ailing transit firms. As shown in Table 7.3, that is what occurred.

The act had a number of other important restrictions, two of which will be discussed in detail later in this chapter. There is, however, one other more subtle yet very significant provision of the 1964 act which should be noted. The act established a federal-local transit partnership, thereby bypassing the state governments. This contrasted with the heavy state involvement in the federal highway program. As a result taxi operators seeking public help in the early 1970s generally found state governments unable to assist them. Only in recent years has the state involvement in transit become more pronounced.

Subsequent to the 1964 act, Congress enacted a number of important amendments. In 1966 it provided planning funds, as well as managerial and research grants. The administration of the federal transit program was switched to the new Department of Transportation in 1968, and long-term and increased funding was established in 1970.

Operating assistance for cities over 50,000 population became available with the passage of the National Mass Transportation Assistance Act of 1974, ten years after the establishment of capital assistance.

The 1974 act again evoked the federal-local partnership: local governments were required to match the federal operating funds. Several states subsequently elected to assist local areas in providing these matching funds, and transit funding became a three-way partnership. The 1974 act did provide for a state role in that operating assistance for cities in the 50,000 to 200,000 population range was passed through state governments.

Operating assistance for cities under 50,000 was not made available until the Surface Transportation Act of 1978. This act was the first joint transit-highways legislation, and true to its multimodal orientation, it made small-city operating assistance a joint responsibility of the Federal Highway Administration (FHWA) and the Urban Mass Transportation Administration (UMTA). Thus, for cities under 50,000, transit funding—both capital and operating—involves FHWA, UMTA, and state governments as key agencies.[7]

This examination of the evolving program of transit assistance yields several conclusions of importance to the taxi industry. First, Congress has deemed transit a federal as well as a local concern. Second, the piecemeal enactment of transit funding has rendered a program that is complex and not easily understood. Third, the transit program does not explicitly deal with either taxicabs or paratransit in general. Finally, the role of state governments has not only changed over time but also varies considerably from state to state. As will be discussed later, these conclusions explain a great deal of the confusion that has accompanied the emergence of paratransit as an element in public transit programs.

## THE DECLINE OF THE FLEETS

The 1970s were not good years for the taxicab industry, particularly for the fleet operators. The size of the industry actually decreased during the decade. More notable, perhaps, the fleet operations declined in relative importance, as some firms went out of business, others became associations of owner-operators, and many others simply became smaller.

While statistics are not available to document the extent of the decline of the fleets, numerous examples exist. One particularly interesting example occurred in New York City. The Haas Act in 1937 had frozen the number of fleet-owned and individual-owned taxi medallions. For decades there had been 6,816 fleet medallions and 4,971 individual medallions. Until about 1966 the price of a fleet medallion was higher than that of an individual medallion. As shown in Table 7.4, that pattern was reversed after 1966, as both types of medallions soared in price, but the individual medallion price stayed consistently higher than the fleet medallion price. In the mid-1970s New York medallion brokers recognized an opportunity to achieve high profits by selling fleet medallions in pairs—thereby legally maintaining them as "fleets"—to individuals. The result was a transfer of about 4,700 fleet medallions to "mini-fleet" operations. While technically still "fleets" in a legal sense, drivers for mini-fleets operate as individual operators. Today, there are only 2,100 fleet medallions, meaning that in one

TABLE 7.4. *Price of New York City Taxi Medallion*

| Year | Individual | Fleet |
|---|---|---|
| 1947 | $ 2,500 | $ 2,500 |
| 1950 | 5,000 | 5,000 |
| 1952 | 7,500 | 7,500 |
| 1959 | 19,500 | 20,000 |
| 1965 | 26,000 | 30,000 |
| 1966 | 25,000 | 18,000 |
| 1968 | 25,000 | 16,000 |
| 1970 | 28,000 | 14,000 |
| 1974 | 30,000 | 18,000 |
| 1976 | 45,000 | 23,000 |
| 1978 | 55,000 | 40,000 |
| 1980 | 68,000 | 55,000 |
| 1981 | 62,000 | 50,000 |

Source: "Trafficking in Taxis," p. 16.

decade the New York taxi industry shifted from 57.8 percent fleet controlled to only 17.8 percent fleet controlled.

In many cities major taxicab fleets declared bankruptcy in the 1970s. Two cases, however, are of particular interest. Philadelphia Yellow Cab, once one of the largest fleets in the country, went bankrupt several years ago. Its path to bankruptcy was not an uncommon one: it postponed maintenance, did not replace worn-out vehicles, and put off paying claims and pension contributions. The remnants of the firm have been sold to a new operator who is attempting to settle the firm's ten million dollars of outstanding claims, an attempt which will include selling 208 of the firm's taxi certificates.

Perhaps the single most illustrative example of the failure of a taxicab fleet was the bankruptcy of the Westgate Corporation and, with it, its taxicab holdings. The taxicab empire assembled by W. Lansing Rothschild was taken over by C. Arnholt Smith's Westgate Corporation in 1962. For many reasons, this "absentee ownership" of the taxi operations did not work well. Westgate required the individual taxi firms to purchase insurance from firms owned by the corporation and subjected the firms to other corporate policies that increased their costs. Contributing to their financial problems was the refusal of the cities to grant needed rate increases. In Los Angeles the general manager of the taxi operation was unable to convince the city to grant a rate increase. He went ahead with the rate increase anyway by changing all of his meters to increase the fares by 5 percent. This illegal action was eventually discovered, and it in no way helped to reverse the declining image of the taxi industry in that city. Finally, in 1976, the entire Westgate Corporation filed for bankruptcy, one of the largest bankruptcy petitions in the history of the United States. In San Francisco and in Los Angeles the former Westgate licenses were scattered among individual owners; the total number of vehicles in each city declined below the levels of the pre-Westgate era.

The reasons for the decline of fleet operations are easy to identify. In the first place the costs of labor, parts, and gasoline all increased rapidly in the 1970s, meaning that fleets—and all operators—were forced to ask for repeated fare increases. Unfortunately for the fleet operators, rate requests always bring adverse attention on fleets because of the size and visibility of their operations. In many cities it was politically impossible to increase fares quickly enough to keep up with rises in costs. Another reason was the competition from government-subsidized transportation services, a factor which will be discussed in detail in later chapters. Still another reason was the increased costs resulting from various employee fringe benefits. Workmen's compensation, Social Security, hospitalization, and pension payments, as well as rising minimum wage standards, all combined to add to the labor costs borne by fleet owners. In addition, unions tried—often successfully—to organize many companies. Already experiencing lower revenues because of competition from government-subsidized services, the fleet operators now faced rising labor costs and, in some cases, union demands for higher commission rates and more restrictive work rules.

For independent owner-operators, these last two factors were of little importance. They had no payrolls, so increases in fringe benefits were irrelevant to them. Likewise, unionization was not a concern. Even the taxes for which they were liable were easily minimized by underreporting their incomes. Government-subsidized competition affected some owner-operators, but for the many independents who directed their services only toward airports and downtown hotels even the government competition was of no concern. The rising cost of gasoline and parts affected all operators, including the owner-operators. Here again, however, the owner-operators were less affected, as fleets not only experienced gas price increases but also lost most if not all of their fleet discounts for bulk purchases. It is not surprising, therefore, that the independents fared better than the fleets in the 1970s and that in New York and other cities nonfleet operations increased at the expense of the fleets.

The effect of unionization on the decline of fleets is impossible to determine. No research has been undertaken showing even the extent of unionization within the industry, much less the consequences of unionization for costs and profits. Moreover, such research would likely miss an important detail: the economic costs to the owners of the many unsuccessful attempts to organize individual fleets. Throughout the country many fleet operators have successfully warded off periodic attempts by several major unions to organize their drivers.

For several reasons unions have not been very successful in organizing the taxi industry. Taxi drivers are often attracted to the industry because of the independence that it offers them. They have some flexibility over the hours they work, and in some cases they can enter and leave their jobs almost at will, meaning that they can experience a certain amount of mobility. They are paid based on the revenues that they generate, which means that they compete with others for fares. More important, however, the taxi industry is too diffused to be organized efficiently. Unlike industries composed of large corporations, the taxi industry is composed of many small firms. Few of these firms are large enough to justify expensive organizing efforts. Moreover, many unions recognize that some cab drivers are moonlighting from another job where they already pay union dues and receive benefits.

The exceptions, of course, are the large fleets in major cities. Chicago Yellow Cab, the world's largest fleet, and Checker Cab, also in Chicago, were organized by the Teamsters in 1937. The first president of the new Teamster Local 777 was Dominic Abata. Internal strife soon occurred, and Abata was deposed by Joseph Glimco, who ran the union efficiently for several years. Abata, however, soon returned. After leaving Chicago to organize a taxi company in St. Louis, Abata returned to Chicago to attempt to organize the taxi drivers into a new local of the Seafarers International Union. After much electioneering, many threats, and some violence, the new Seafarers local, called the Democratic Union Organizing Committee, prevailed. In July 1975 both Chicago companies decided to lease vehicles to drivers who wished to do so. This threat to the power of the union was met by a court suit brought by the union to prevent leasing. In June 1979, the Court of Appeals for the District of Columbia upheld an administrative law judge's ruling in favor of the taxi companies. The result has been a major decrease in union membership, as many drivers have become lessee-drivers and therefore are no longer "employees."

The experience in New York City has been similar. Rogoff reports that taxi drivers there were the subject of union organizing attempts as early as 1915.[8] The first successful organization attempt occurred in 1937 when the Transport Workers Union (TWU) won recognition and negotiated with the twenty-eight fleets. TWU representation was to last only two years, and the TWU abandoned its attempt to organize taxi drivers in 1947. Several other unions, including the United Mine Workers in 1949, also tried to organize the New York taxi industry. Finally, in 1965, Harry Van Arsdale's Taxi Drivers Union succeeded in organizing the fleet drivers and recently has agreed to help the large fleets by allowing them to lease vehicles.[9] However, large fleets have greatly declined in number because of the switch of fleet medallions to minifleet operators. The decline in taxi fleets and the trend toward leasing among the fleet owners have combined to erode the strength of the taxi union.

## FEDERAL TRANSIT POLICY AND THE TAXI INDUSTRY

By the mid-1970s as traditional exclusive-ride taxi service was becoming more unprofitable, federal transportation policy placed the taxi industry in a financial position not unlike that which private urban bus operators had faced a decade earlier. Publicly subsidized transportation services were competing directly for services that could be more efficiently provided by taxi operators under contract to public agencies. Yet federal transit programs had not been written to allow for the use of taxis in such instances. Both taxi operators and public officials were unsure whether taxicabs were eligible for UMTA funds. Nor did taxi operators know if they had any legal protection against the expenditure of public funds on services that competed with them. The lack of definitive answers for these two crucial questions is an indication of the confusion that prevailed in transportation policy.

A small example might illustrate this confusion. The Highway Act of 1973 added section 16 to the 1964 Urban Mass Transportation Act. Section 16 provided UMTA funding to "private non-profit corporations and associations" for the purchase of vehicles to serve the transportation needs of the elderly and handicapped. That these special mobility needs should be addressed within public transit programs has never been an issue of debate. What has been debated is how these special needs should be met. Section 16 provides for one mechanism: public funds to purchase vehicles for nonprofit agencies. No mention was made in the act of including taxi operators; nor was

*Morris Markin shown with a Checker cab in 1970. (Collection of the author.)*

any provision included to protect or compensate taxi operators for business lost to the services provided by these publicly purchased vehicles.

The result was predictable. After about $20 million was expended in fiscal year 1975 under section 16, taxi operators protested to UMTA officials on the grounds of unfair competition. In January 1976 the UMTA administrator issued new guidelines for administering section 16. These required a nonprofit agency to obtain a sign-off from "each public and private transit and paratransit operator in the service area" indicating agreement with the agency's request for section 16 funds. Alternatively, the guidelines allowed the agency to publish a public notice inviting operators to comment on the request. While not perfect, the guidelines have helped protect the rights of private operators at least to know about section 16 grants.

The example of section 16 grants illustrates the difficulties encountered in attempting to include paratransit services in program and policies designed solely for transit systems. Much time, expense, and ill will were expended in attempting to include the taxi industry in the section 16 program—or to protect taxi operators from the program. In this case public policy was modified to include the taxi industry. In other more important policy areas these modifications have not yet been made.

One such policy area is the question of whether taxicabs and paratransit services in general are eligible for federal transit funds. Section 12c-6 of the Urban Mass Transportation Act defines "mass transportation" as "transportation by bus, or rail, or other conveyance, either publicly or privately owned, which provides to the public general or special service . . . on a regular and continuing basis." This definition neither mentions taxicabs specifically nor rules them out. Certain taxi services could be included under the words *other conveyance*. The definition also makes privately owned services eligible. The question is whether taxi services are "available to the public . . . on a regular and continuing basis." A liberal interpretation of this provision would include taxi services of all kinds, since they are in fact available to the public. A more restrictive interpretation is that a vehicle that can be reserved by a single passenger for his or her exclusive use is no longer available to the "public." This second interpretation means that only shared-ride taxi services fall within the UMTA definition of mass transportation.

Setting aside for a moment these definitional questions, the Urban Mass Transportation Act still includes two restrictions that deserve further scrutiny. Sections 3e and 13c were both put into the act in 1964 and were intended to apply to the public takeover of privately owned transit firms. They still apply, however, to federal transit funding, and if taxicab services are "mass transportation," then they apply to taxicabs as well as transit.

Section 13c has occasioned more discussion and controversy than any provision in the Urban Mass Transportation Act. It is a simple provision, reading in part: "It should be a condition under Section 3 of this Act that fair and equitable arrangements are made, as determined by the Secretary of Labor, to protect the interests of employees affected by such assistance." At first glance, this provision seems uncontroversial; certainly employee rights and benefits, such as collective bargaining rights, should not be lost because of the expenditure of federal funds. However, section 13c does not specify what "fair and equitable arrangements" are or under what condition the secretary of labor shall approve of these arrangements. In practice, in all but a few cases, the secretary of labor has granted approval if the local transit union has first approved of the arrangements for protecting employee rights.

While much has been written about the effects of section 13c on transit costs and innovation, its effects on the taxi industry have received far less attention. If a taxi firm is to be considered a mass transportation provider, a firm's employees must somehow be protected under section 13c. This protection becomes more problematic when one remembers that many taxicab drivers are independent contractors and that drivers employed by firms are often not represented by the same union that represents transit employees. Thus, even identifying someone at the local level who can assure the secretary of labor that section 13c protection has been provided can be difficult.

The questions involving section 13c and taxicab firms have been partially answered in several recent rulings by the Department of Labor. A 1977 UMTA grant to the Port Authority for Allegheny County drew a protest from the Pittsburgh taxi industry. Responding to the labor questions in this protest, the Department of Labor found that 15 percent or more of the business of one of the taxi firms was shared-ride service, and the department included the employees providing such services within section 13c protection. A similar finding occurred in a more recent case in New Haven, Connecticut. With these cases as precedents, the department has included among several criteria the requirement that 15 percent of revenues must come from shared-ride services in order for a taxi firm's employees to be included within the provisions of section 13c. In addition, even if a firm does not meet the 15-percent requirement, an individual driver may receive such protection if he provides a significant amount of shared-ride service.

The issues surrounding section 13c are far from being resolved, but they have already taught the taxi industry two important lessons. One is that to be considered a mass transportation provider a taxi firm needs to provide shared-ride service; apparently, at least 15 percent of its revenue must be shared-ride business. Second, section 13c coverage for taxi drivers may provide a legal mechanism for taxi service to be included in local transit funding programs.

While section 13c protects employees, section 3e protects firms. It states in part: "No financial assistance shall be provided . . . for the operation of mass transportation facilities or equipment in competition with, or supplementary to, the service provided by an existing mass transportation company, unless" four conditions are met. One of those is that "the Secretary finds that such programs, to the maximum extent feasible, provide for the participation of private mass transportation companies." Here again the question arises whether a taxi firm is a "mass transportation company." If so, then local services planned and implemented without the participation of local taxi firms would be illegal. Thus section 3e provides potentially valuable legal protection for taxi firms if they can be considered mass transportation providers. This condition presumably means that they provide a substantial amount of shared-ride service.

Attempting to clarify these issues, UMTA published a proposed paratransit policy in the *Federal Register* for 20 October 1976. This two-page statement specified that paratransit services would be eligible for federal transit funding if they were shared-ride services and that a firm would be eligible if more than an incidental portion of its business was derived from such shared-ride services. It also defined "maximum feasible participation of private operators" to exist if such providers were given an opportunity to bid on paratransit services. This proposed policy was a much-needed attempt to clarify the policy confusion that surrounded the involvement of taxi firms in federal transit programs; however, it has never become finalized. The Reagan administration has, however, promised to issue a paratransit statement, as well as a regulation concerning section 3e. Perhaps these documents will alleviate the uncertainty concerning the role of taxicab operators in federal programs.

## PUBLIC INVOLVEMENT: A NEW ERA

Although the increase of public involvement in transportation issues in the 1960s and 1970s directly affected taxi operators in some ways—such as in fuel allocation rules—its major influence was more subtle and more indirect, but nonetheless pervasive. Through fiscal year 1978 in the transit program alone the federal government had spent $10.3 billion on operating assistance.[10] In addition the federal government had established several programs to provide subsidized services for transportation-disadvantaged persons. In the period of about fifteen years the local transportation environment had completely changed, as, bit by bit, program by program, public expenditures and associated program guidelines and procedures proliferated.

It is tempting to try to measure the effects of federal programs in quantitative terms, such as dollars and passengers. Taxicab operators have argued convincingly that public expenditures for local transportation services have cut deeply into their revenues. Such measures are illusive, however. Taxicab ridership changes in response to many factors, and it is nearly impossible to determine what portion of such shifts should be ascribed to specific public expenditures. Moreover, some of this money, particularly from the human service programs, has been used to purchase taxicab services. Thus, the economic costs of federal transit programs to the taxi industry, while no doubt real, are not subject to reliable estimation.

Irrespective of these economic costs, these federal programs have had other important effects. Simply put, the infusion of public funds into local transportation has greatly altered how taxi firms operate. Whereas, in most instances, taxi operators formerly dealt only with local city councils, they must now deal with numerous public agencies at all levels of government. This involvement has meant many more meetings, written reports, and letters, all of which absorb time formerly devoted to other management functions. Taxi operators have also been taught by the section 13c rulings that they should increase their shared-ride business. Involvement in human service programs has shown them the need for detailed operational data, as well as the costs of waiting several months for payments. Finally, taxi operators have discovered the need for public relations in order to survive in the new political environment in which they find themselves.

The full impact of the increased federal involvement has yet to be completely felt or understood. What is clear is that the 1960s and 1970s can be viewed as a time which moved the taxicab from relative political isolation into intense involvement in the public sector.

# 8

# THE ECONOMICS OF TAXICAB OPERATIONS

As a private, nonsubsidized carrier, the taxi industry depends upon its ability to generate revenues in excess of its costs. Its survival depends on this ability. For taxicab operators, therefore, economics has a realistic and essential quality.

## THE ORGANIZATION OF THE INDUSTRY

Taxi firms are organized in three ways: employee-driver, lessee-driver, and owner-driver. The employee-driver drives a car that is owned by the company, and he is usually paid on a commission basis. The key element of this arrangement is the employer-employee relationship, which requires that the employer guarantee the driver a minimum hourly wage and pay Social Security taxes, payroll taxes, and other benefits. Commissions are usually in the range of 43 to 50 percent; with the addition of fringe benefits payroll costs amount to over 50 percent of revenues for employee-driver operations.

The lessee-driver and owner-driver arrangements avoid the employer-employee arrangement by making the driver, in effect, an independent contractor. Under a lease arrangement, a driver will pay a daily, weekly, or monthly fee for the use of a vehicle. An owner-driver owns his or her vehicle. Under either the lessee-driver or owner-driver arrangement, the driver may contract with the firm for such services as advertising, fuel, dispatching, and maintenance.

One special case of the owner-driver firm is the single-taxi firm, sometimes called an "independent" or "owner-operator firm." These firms exist in many cities and represent a very different type of taxi operation. Owner-operators, particularly those not belonging to some type of cooperative dispatching arrangement, depend almost entirely on street-hail business, and they focus primarily on high-density locations, such as airports and hotels. Since these operators rarely join the International Taxicab Association and seldom respond to surveys of the industry, little is known about the scope and economics of their operations; national estimates of the size of the taxi industry, therefore, are conservative in that owner-operators are undercounted. Moreover, in cities with open entry into the taxi industry independent operators may constitute a transient segment of the local industry in that they may continually enter and leave the taxi business.

In many cases, however, owner-operators form local associations in order to purchase fuel and tires in bulk quantities and to establish cooperative dispatching services. At one extreme, these associations may be very loosely organized, with each cab painted a different color and operating under a different name. At the other extreme, an association may be highly organized and, in essence, be a firm which is cooperatively owned. In one "service company" arrangement in Seattle, owner-operators purchase dispatching and maintenance from a cooperatively owned company.

Not only are the distinctions between the various organizational forms somewhat ambiguous, but also they change over time. Checker Taxi of Chicago began as a loosely organized association of very independent owner-operators, and it later became a highly centralized fleet operation. Fleet companies in other cities have also descended from associations. Today, however, although some fleet operators are purchasing independent owner-operators, the trend is toward reducing the fleets in favor of owner-driver or lessee-driver arrangements. Firms are frequently combinations of all three types of vehicle ownership, and the percentages of each type may be continually changing in any one firm.

There is an important economic reason why operators have switched to lessee- or owner-driver arrangements. A lessee-driver or an owner-driver is an independent contractor and, as such, is not entitled to such employee benefits as Social Security, workmen's compensation, and hospitalization. In addition, independent contractors are seldom unionized in the taxi business. Not only do these cost savings accrue to the firm but also the operators greatly reduce their record-keeping and payroll-withholding responsibilities.

It is in the legal definition of "independent contractor" that taxi operators experience a disadvantage when they switch to lessee-driver or owner-driver management arrangements. Recent court cases and current IRS policy distinguish independent contractors as persons over whom the taxi operator has no direct control. This definition puts the taxi operator in a dilemma: lessee-driver arrangements would reduce payroll costs, but the operator would lose control over when and how a driver works. Some operators have maintained that this is a phony dilemma in that they never had control over their drivers even when the drivers were employees. Other operators, however, find the prospect of no direct control to be contrary to their management philosophies. Still other operators have switched to leasing while pushing for local ordinance changes to increase the municipal control over drivers. Close municipal regulation produces the same control as does the employer-employee relationship.

Because of the economic advantages, it is likely that more firms will switch to leasing and owner-driver arrangements. In fact there is evidence that the switch to leasing is already underway. Wells's surveys of the taxi industry show that the percentage of lease operations increased from 7.7 percent in 1973 to 12.0 percent in 1975.[1] However, the small response rates in both years preclude any firm interpretation of those figures.[2] Actually, the trend toward leasing began in earnest after 1975 and hence is not reflected in Wells's results.

Table 8.1 presents the percentages for all types of firms for the two Wells surveys. Again, the small samples no doubt distort the results, particularly for 1975. It is apparent, however, that the employee-driver firm is by far the most prevalent type. It also seems that the number of owner-driver firms decreased markedly during the two years. It must be remembered, however, that this category includes one-vehicle firms, which are the most difficult ones for which to obtain data. The decrease, therefore, may be due to particularly low response rates for this group in 1975.

Sampling problems notwithstanding, these data raise questions regarding the future organization of the industry. Earlier chapters have

TABLE 8.1. *Taxicab Firms by Type*

| Type of Firm | 1973 (percent) | 1975 (percent) |
|---|---|---|
| Employee-driver only | 66.3 | 71.2 |
| Lessee-driver only | 7.7 | 12.0 |
| Owner-driver only | 11.2 | 0.8 |
| Employee and lessee | 3.4 | 8.0 |
| Employee and owner | 5.7 | 4.8 |
| Lessee and owner | 2.3 | 1.6 |
| Employee, lessee, and owner | 3.4 | 1.6 |

Source: Wells, "Taxicab Operating."

shown that the taxi industry and its predecessors have used all of these organizational forms since the days of the hackneys in England. It is likely—and Wells's results agree—that taxi firms will continue to switch among these management forms.

From a public policy standpoint the instability and variation in management forms work against the industry in one important way. Public officials who wish to involve taxi operators in publicly funded paratransit programs are often confused by the variety of types and sizes of taxi firms. Serious problems arise in ensuring that each firm is given an equal chance to bid on these services. For example, some public agencies are wary of contracting with a firm whose drivers are independent contractors. They perceive that such firms may not be able to exercise control over the drivers and therefore may not be able to provide consistent, high-quality service. How the industry responds to such a perception—how firms organize and how successful operators are in explaining those organizational forms—is an important indicator of how successful the industry will be participating in public transportation programs.

## INDUSTRY STRUCTURE

The taxi industry is made up of a large number of separate firms. In 1975 the International Taxicab Association had a mailing list of 5,387 firms. Only a handful of these operated more than one taxi company. With few exceptions, taxi operations are locally owned and operated.

Within the industry the firms vary widely in size. As shown in Table 8.2, small firms overwhelm the large firms in number, but the few large firms account for most of the passengers.

There is reason to believe that the true distribution of firm size is more skewed toward the small firms. The Wells surveys had very low response rates among small firms, and many small firms may not even have received a questionnaire. Inventories of taxi firms conducted on a state basis in several states have shown much higher percentages of small firms. For example, in North Carolina 90 percent of the firms in a 1978 study were found to have fewer than ten cabs.[3] Inventories of firms in Wisconsin, New Mexico, and Ohio have yielded percentages of 90 percent, 85 percent, and 69 percent, respectively,[4] for this class of firms. The taxi industry is apparently much more a "mom-and-pop" industry than was shown in the Wells surveys.

TABLE 8.2. *Distribution of Firm Sizes for United States*

| Number of Taxis in Firm | Percentage of Firms | | Percentage of Passengers | |
|---|---|---|---|---|
| | 1973 | 1975 | 1973 | 1975 |
| Under 10 | 36.0 | 24.9 | 5.1 | 3.0 |
| 10–24 | 31.0 | 37.1 | 14.8 | 14.2 |
| 25–49 | 15.1 | 15.9 | 13.1 | 10.3 |
| 50–74 | 7.4 | 9.4 | 10.2 | 11.0 |
| 75–99 | 4.3 | 4.9 | 9.4 | 13.1 |
| 100–199 | 3.5 | 3.7 | 10.9 | 6.5 |
| 200 or more | 2.7 | 4.1 | 36.5 | 41.9 |

Source: Wells, "Taxicab Operating."

The importance of the smaller taxi firms extends well beyond statistical data. They operate in low-density areas and in small cities, which often have little or no public transit services. They are operated by people who work long hours for little money and keep overhead expenses to a minimum by operating bus depots, snack bars, restaurants, gas stations, or other businesses out of the buildings that house their taxi businesses. They serve a needy clientele at a fraction of the cost that a similar publicly owned service would incur. Large firms naturally serve more people, but the small firms provide a service that is no less vital. Unfortunately, it is the small firm which is in the greatest financial jeopardy and for which survival is a day-to-day struggle.

## SUPPLY CHARACTERISTICS

A basic consideration in any analysis of taxi economics is that of supply: To what extent are taxis available, and is taxi supply increasing or decreasing? To answer such questions, measurements of taxi supply are necessary.

No available measure accurately represents taxi supply. A true measure of supply would be the number of vehicle-hours of service actually provided. While it is possible to collect data on vehicle-hours, available data sources do not include this measure. Some studies have examined the hours per day that taxi firms operate, but this measure does not reflect variations in the number of taxis on the streets at any given time throughout the day. One is left with the problem of making inferences based upon inadequate supply measures.

There are several supply measures: the number of taxis; the number of vehicle-miles; the number of cities with taxi service; and the number of taxi firms. The most common measure, however, is the ratio of population to taxis or to taxi licenses. This measure has the advantages of being easily estimated and city size can be controlled for. Thus, it is a convenient measure for comparing taxi operations in two or more cities.

The variations in this measure from city to city are extreme. Table 8.3 shows the results from several studies that have measured taxi

TABLE 8.3. *Taxi Supply Characteristics*

| Area | Sample | Persons per License | | Persons per Taxi | |
|---|---|---|---|---|---|
| | | Median | Mean | Median | Mean |
| Pennsylvania | 29 cities | | | 1,654 | 2,102 |
| North Carolina | 8 small cities | 714 | | 794 | |
| Illinois | 6 counties | | | 4,762 | 2,857 |
| Wisconsin | 13 urban areas | | | 3,195 | 4,101 |
| United States | 741 cities | 1,760 | 1,078 | | |
| United States | 30 large cities | 1,176 | 662 | | |

Source: Brown, "Economic Analysis"; Gilbert et al., "Taxicab User"; Northeastern Illinois Planning Commission, "Taxicabs and Dial-a-Bus"; Wisconsin Department of Transportation, "Wisconsin Taxicabs"; Webster et al., "Role of Taxicabs"; and Kirby et al., *Paratransit*.

supply. While the means and medians in the table show large variations between the studies, the ratios vary even more on a city-by-city basis.

However, it is impossible to make any but the most general inferences from such ratios. Differences in these ratios may be caused by a variety of factors. For example, a city with many owner-operator taxis will tend to have an unrealistically high population-taxi ratio because of an underestimation of the total number of taxis. Using the number of licenses in the ratio alleviates this problem only for cities in which the license data are reliable and all licenses are held by active cabs. Neither ratio corrects for a deficiency which is even more serious: the daily variation in taxis. Because more taxis operate early in the month in small cities, the taxi supply varies accordingly. A true measure of taxi supply would also vary, but such a measure must await better data.

These problems notwithstanding, the ratio of population to licenses is still the best available supply measure. As a measure to compare two or more cities, these ratios are useful only at a general level. However, as a longitudinal measure for a single city, they are more informative:

they provide a method of determining changes over time in the supply of taxi service.

Another longitudinal measure is simply the number of taxi licenses, a statistic sometimes available on a state-wide basis. For example, in North Carolina the number of taxicabs decreased by 22.9 percent between 1970 and 1977.[5] The United States Census Bureau's *County Business Patterns* includes estimates of taxi firms—not vehicles—and shows a 25.1 percent decrease in firms from 1964 to 1972. The International Taxicab Association file of taxi firms decreased by 16.7 percent from 1974 to 1976. These figures on firms are obviously not a direct measure of taxi supply. Better data on the number of taxis on a state-by-state basis over time are unfortunately not available.

## DEMAND CHARACTERISTICS

Economic survival for a taxicab firm depends on ridership. Three aspects of demand are of particular importance: the level of demand, the persons who use taxis, and the trips for which taxis are used.

### LEVEL OF DEMAND

Demand for taxi service can be measured by either trips served or passengers carried. The two Wells surveys of the national taxicab industry found that the mean number of annual passengers per taxi decreased from 11,900 in 1973 to 10,300 in 1975. Busath found a slightly higher mean of 13,195 annual passengers per taxi in a survey of fifty-one California firms.[6] However, the variation in this measure from firm to firm is extreme. In the California sample the annual passengers per taxi ranged from 2,000 to 31,646. The Wells survey for 1975 found that one-fourth of the firms carried fewer than 7,900 annual passengers per cab, while another one-fourth reported carrying over 17,300 per cab.

Similar variations exist with another demand measure, trips per thousand population. The Northeastern Illinois Planning Commission (NIPC) computed taxi trips per thousand population for subareas within a six-county region in northeastern Illinois.[7] Although controlling for population, this measure varied widely from the most urban subareas (8,644 for the Loop) to the most rural (4.6 for an outer suburban ring). Excluding the Loop, the mean value for the suburban region was 79.4 trips per thousand population.

The variations in these demand indicators result from several factors; not the least of these is the fact that individual operators may or may not include part-time taxis when reporting their operating data. A better measure of demand would use "taxi-hours" rather than "taxis" in the denominator. However, data on taxi-hours are not reported.

It is possible that some of the variations in demand measures are not attributable to reporting inconsistencies. Rather, these variations may be more systematic: that is, various sizes of firms or cities may generate different levels of demand on a per-taxi or per-capita basis. Some evidence exists to support this suggestion. Wells, for example, found in 1976 that firms with seventy-five to ninety-nine taxis generate the highest demand while firms with one hundred to two hundred cabs generate the lowest.[8] Likewise, the NIPC found that population is correlated with taxi trips per capita. However, taxi trip generation has not been subjected to the same intense analysis as have auto trips; thus, it remains unclear to what extent population, population density, income, firm size, and other variables influence the level of taxi demand.

Less variation exists in a related variable. Trips and persons are related by the occupancy rate, or persons per trip, a measure which indicates the degree of group riding that occurs. As shown in Table 8.4, the variation in the occupancy rate between taxi surveys is slight; approximately one and one-half persons per trip is the consistent result. Given that taxis can carry at least five passengers, this rate demonstrates that taxis operating in an exclusive-ride mode have unused capacity.

### PASSENGER CHARACTERISTICS

Two groups predominate among taxi users. In large cities some persons use taxis by choice. These users include businessmen and high-income persons who have cars but use taxis for convenience. Table

TABLE 8.4. *Taxi Occupancy Rate*

| Area | Reference | Mean Passengers per Trip |
|---|---|---|
| Pennsylvania | Brown (1973) | 1.61 |
| North Carolina | Gilbert et al. (1976) | 1.45 |
| California | Busath (1975) | 1.74 |
| United States | Wells (1975) | 1.60 |
| United States | Wells (1977) | 1.46 |

8.5, which shows trip and user characteristics from taxi studies, documents the existence of large percentages of upper-income taxi users.

The second large group of taxi users is composed of low-income or otherwise taxi-dependent persons. As demonstrated in Table 8.5, this group is more dominant in smaller cities. For example, Gilbert et al. found that in small North Carolina cities users of taxis were almost entirely taxi dependent.[9] Relatively few taxi users in these cities had a car, a driver's license, or an income over ten thousand dollars. Instead, over half the taxi users in the North Carolina sample earned less than five thousand dollars per year.

These results point to the need for a careful examination of those already using taxis when contemplating taxi innovations. Because of the extreme variations in income between taxi users, specific policies regarding fare levels can have drastically different impacts on the various user groups. More important, these user characteristics suggest the need for taxi operators to offer a variety of types of services at different fare levels.

TRIP CHARACTERISTICS

The purposes of taxi trips are also shown in Table 8.5. Again, a difference between large and small cities is observable. The smaller cities (for example, those in the North Carolina sample) have higher percentages using taxis for shopping and lower percentages using them to get to work. This difference reflects the greater taxi dependence of the small city taxi user. Conversely, in larger cities more taxi trips are work related because of the greater employment concentrations, the higher number of business visitors, and the increased difficulty of finding parking.

Not unexpectedly, the lengths of taxi trips vary with both city size and trip purpose. Here an important distinction must be made between total miles and paid miles. One common measure of trip length is computed by dividing total annual miles by total trips. This figure is misleading in that it includes deadhead miles; the more appropriate measure of trip length is paid miles per trip.

Estimates of trip length vary considerably. Busath estimated the mean trip length for fifty-one California firms to be 3.68 paid miles.[10] The NIPC estimated the mean trip length for all taxi trips in northeastern Illinois to be 2.8 airline miles.[11] Wells found that the mean trip length for his 1975 national sample of taxi firms was 2.85 paid miles.[12] Moreover, he found that the length of taxi trips increases with firm size, from 2.12 miles for the smallest firms to 3.02 miles for firms with two hundred or more cabs. It seems reasonable to assume that firm size is correlated strongly with city size, implying that larger firms experience longer trip lengths because they serve larger areas.

## FARES

Taxi fares are computed in a variety of ways, depending upon local taxi ordinances. There are, however, three primary fare structures: meter fares, zone fares, and flat fares. In addition, some operators use more than one of these fare structures, either in combination or at different times.

Meter fares consist of a drop charge and a per-mile fee. Wells found that the typical drop charge in 1975 was about seventy to eighty cents per 1.6 miles.[13] The typical mileage charge was ten cents per 1/6 mile. In addition, 54.1 percent of the firms operated a "live clock": that is, they charged for time delayed in traffic. In California in 1975 over 63 percent of the operators used a live clock.[14]

TABLE 8.5. *Characteristics of Taxi Users and Taxi Trips (percentages)*

| Area | Female | House-wives | No Car | No License | Over 60 Years | Nonwhite | Employee |
|---|---|---|---|---|---|---|---|
| Chicago | 58.8 | 45.0 | | 31.9 males<br>71.2 females | 6.7 males<br>5.3 females | 9.8 | |
| Northeastern Illinois | 46.0 | 18.0 | | | 12.0 | 19.0 | 69.0 |
| North Carolina | 63.7<br>64.7 | 12.9<br>12.2 | 58.2<br>56.3 | 74.7<br>70.6 | 23.3<br>17.6 | 61.1<br>63.7 | 55.2<br>58.1 |
| Pittsburgh (1970) | 61.0 | | 52.0 | 42.0 | | | |
| Pittsburgh (1963) | | 34.0 | | 48.0 males<br>75.0 females | | | |
| Hicksville | 68.5<br>72.0 | 23.4<br>28.1 | 8.8<br>12.0 | 56.2<br>66.0 | 4.3<br>2.0 | | 72.0<br>63.9 |
| Davenport | 66.7<br>72.1 | 24.1<br>19.7 | 35.4<br>48.0 | 61.5<br>59.6 | 14.4<br>14.0 | | 61.3<br>65.9 |
| United States | 51.1 | | | | 21.7 | | |
| Denver | | | | | 6.4 | 24.2 | |

Source: Gilbert et al., "Taxicab User," pp. 8–9.

Economics / 115

| | Income | | | Trip Purpose | | | |
| Professionals, Technicians, Managers | Under $3000 | Under $5000 | Over $10,000 | Work | Shopping | Social Recreation | Medical |
|---|---|---|---|---|---|---|---|
| 48.4 | | | | | | | |
| | 8.0 | | 71.0 ($9000) | | | | |
| 13.1 | 33.3 | 54.3 | 15.2 | 20.5 | 37.0 | 16.0 | 7.6 |
| 14.2 | 30.0 | 52.4 | 18.2 | 23.5 | 36.4 | 15.2 | 6.8 |
| | | | | | | | |
| 44.8 | | | | | | | |
| | | 6.2 | 72.9 | 56.1 | 19.0 | 7.2 | 5.9 |
| | | 30.2 | 38.6 | 49.3 | 9.0 | 13.3 | 15.6 |
| | 17.7 | 25.3 | 22.2 | 32.0 | 16.3 | 12.0 | 16.7 |
| | | 12.7 ($6000) | 48.9 ($12000) | 22.8 | 8.6 | 18.5 | 9.9 |

Zone fares and flat fares can be charged in several ways. The most common zone fare scheme includes an initial charge for the first zone and a second charge for each zone that has to be entered in order to get to the destination. The fare is computed using a straight line from origin to destination rather than the actual route taken by the taxi. In some cases, however, the per-zone fare varies from zone to zone to reflect different traffic conditions in each zone. Finally, some operators use flat fares, particularly for specific trips, such as trips to airports. In essence, a flat fare is a special case of a zone fare.

The predominant fare system is the meter fare. Wells found that 71 percent of taxi operators in 1975 used meters either entirely or in combination with another fare scheme, and 47.2 percent used meters only.[15] Other estimates are even higher: Busath found that 95.7 percent of the California operators used meters,[16] and the NIPC reported that 80 percent of the operators in northeastern Illinois used meters.[17] In the Wells survey 16.2 reported using zones only and 5.2 used only flat rates.[18]

Regardless of the fare system, the cost of a taxi trip remains a primary concern. In 1975 the International Taxicab Association found that in forty-six United States cities the cost of a three-mile trip ranged from $1.70 to $3.10, with a mean cost of $2.54 for a similar trip, or an 11.9 percent increase over fares of two years earlier.[19] In September 1981 the three-mile fare for the twelve most populous cities averaged $3.56.[20]

This difference in costs between a one-mile trip and a three-mile trip suggests that fare structure is an important policy variable. The Wells survey showed that the fare for the first mile of a taxi trip tends to be twice that for either the second or third mile.[21] This higher initial cost—reflecting the drop charge for meter fares—is justified by the need to cover the cost of deadhead miles. While this need is real, it is also true that the typical taxi fare structure penalizes shorter trips. An alternative approach would be to lower per-mile fares for shorter trips with the expectation that the higher demand would decrease the deadhead miles. This approach is being followed by a number of operators offering dial-a-ride services.

The opposite approach was adopted in 1979 by Dallas. That city perceived a lack of adequate taxi service for short trips in downtown

Dallas. After studying the profitability of short and long taxi trips, the city increased the drop charge from $.65 to $1.30 so as to make short trips more profitable and thereby divert taxis from the airport to the downtown.

Another aspect of fare structures which has important policy ramifications is the charge for additional passengers. Without extra charges for more than one passenger, group riding can make taxi usage dramatically more economical. For example, consider the per-passenger cost of a taxi trip. Given Wells's estimate of a mean fare paid in 1975 of $2.23, a party of four persons would each pay $.56. However, the actual mean occupancy rate estimated by Wells for 1975 was only 1.46, making the mean per-passenger cost of a taxi trip to be $1.53. Gilbert et al. found a lower per-passenger mean fare of $1.19 for smaller cities.[22] These figures suggest that the public is not aware of the cost savings of group riding in taxis which do not have charges for additional passengers. They also suggest that taxi operators have been remiss in not marketing taxi service on a per-passenger cost basis.

## TAXI REVENUES

Lacking public subsidies, taxicabs must depend on operating revenues to cover costs. Revenues depend on local fare structures and levels of demand. As has already been shown, both of these factors vary considerably from city to city. It is not surprising, therefore, that revenues also vary widely.

To control for firm size, it is necessary to express revenues on a per-taxi, per-trip, or per-mile basis. A taxicab generated about $15,000 to $17,000 per year in revenue in 1975. Actually, Wells found that the mean value in 1975 was $17,400 and the median was $15,400,[23] and Busath found a mean of $15,374 for California firms.[24] However, the variation in this value is large. In the California sample the per-taxi annual revenues ranged from $4,000 to $33,000. In the survey by Wells fully one-fourth of the operators reported per-taxi revenues of less than $11,300, while another one-fourth reported revenues over $20,400.[25]

Similar variations exist in per-trip and per-mile revenues. Gilbert et al. found a mean per-trip revenue of $1.72 for small cities in North Carolina.[26] This figure agrees well with Wells's results, which show the mean per-trip revenue to increase from $1.31 for the smallest firms to $2.68 for firms with two hundred or more cabs.[27] The mean for Wells's sample is $2.23, and the median is $1.97. Using either paid miles or total miles in the denominator produces a similar variation from small to large firms. Wells's results show that the smallest firms in 1975 received $.37 per total mile and $.63 per paid mile, while the largest firms received $.47 and $.89. On the basis of total miles the mean was $.43 and the median was $.41. For paid miles, the mean was $.83 and the median $.82.

## COSTS

The availability of cost data is limited. While most operators carefully monitor their costs, they are seldom required to furnish these cost data on a regular basis to public agencies. Thus, the best and most comprehensive cost estimates available are based on voluntary data submissions to the International Taxicab Association from individual operators. The most recent cost data are shown in Table 8.6. The impact of inflation is obvious, as the per-mile costs have increased 83 percent from 1975 to 1979. These figures are highly aggregated; individual terms may deviate substantially from these figures. For example, Wells found that in 1975 the mean cost per vehicle-mile varied from 31 cents for the smallest firms to 43 cents for the largest firms.[28]

A study of the taxicab industry in the Dallas–Fort Worth area documents the recent increases in operating costs.[29] Between 1978 and 1979 the average cost of operating a taxi in the Dallas–Fort Worth area increased from 53.1 cents to 69.3 cents per mile, an increase of 31 percent in only one year. Of this increase, 2.6 cents per mile was attributable to fuel cost increases. The average fuel cost per taxi was between $1,160 and $1,350 higher for 1979 than for 1978.

Cost-per-hour data are more scarce. Shared-ride taxi firms in Hicksville, New York, and Davenport, Iowa, in 1974 averaged $4.78

TABLE 8.6. *Operating Costs (cents per mile)*

|  | 1972 | 1975 | 1978 | 1979 |
|---|---|---|---|---|
| Driver labor | 17.69 | 19.02 | 22.0 | 26.0 |
| Other labor | 1.44 | 2.31 | 3.0 | 7.2 |
| Tires | .28 | .39 | .5 | .8 |
| Parts | .78 | 1.51 | 2.0 | 2.6 |
| Gasoline | 2.29 | 4.47 | 5.0 | 8.1 |
| Insurance | 1.76 | 2.31 | 3.0 | 3.4 |
| Depreciation | 1.50 | 1.87 | 2.0 | 2.8 |
| Dispatching | 5.02 | 5.13 | 6.0 | 4.4 |
| Miscellaneous | — | — | — | 7.9 |
| Total | 30.31 | 37.01 | 43.5 | 63.2 |

Source: International Taxicab Association.

and $4.17 per vehicle-hour, respectively.[30] These figures are probably close to the national average. Webster, Wells, and Weiner report a mean taxi speed of 12.05 miles per hour, which at a 1975 cost of $.41 per mile equals $4.94 per vehicle-hour.[31]

By contrast, the NIPC reports the hourly costs for twelve bus dial-a-ride systems: the median is $9.40 and the range is from $6.65 to $14.43.[32] These comparisons confirm claims made by taxi operators that they can offer dial-a-ride at one-third to one-half the cost of bus dial-a-ride systems.

## PROFITABILITY

Given the cost and revenue figures presented here, it is not surprising to find the taxi industry in a difficult financial condition. The mean cost per trip in 1975 was $2.15, while the mean revenue was $2.23.[33] While this difference means that the industry as a whole realized a profit, the small size of this difference implies that many individual firms did not. Wells's findings confirm this inference. He estimates that one-half of the firms did not generate enough revenues to cover operating and depreciation costs, while one out of four firms did not even cover their operating costs.[34] This ominous finding contrasts sharply with 1970 figures, which showed the median operating ratio to be 83.7 percent or over eleven percentage points better than 1975. Only one-fourth of the firms in Wells's survey in 1975 were as profitable as the industry-wide median for 1970.

Wells's results further show scale effects with respect to firm size. Table 8.7 shows that the operating ratio varies with firm size. The ratios in Table 8.7 do not include depreciation costs, which have been shown to be over 6 percent of total costs. According to the table the most profitable firms are those with seventy-five to ninety-nine cabs.

## PERFORMANCE MEASURES

A variety of measures can be used to monitor the performance of a taxi firm or firms. Some of these measure various types of efficiency, while others measure such characteristics as demand and service quality. Of primary importance, however, are those measuring profitability.

TABLE 8.7. *Operating Ratios Excluding Depreciation Costs*

| Number of Cabs in Fleet | Costs as a Percentage of Revenues |
|---|---|
| 1–9 | 88.8 |
| 10–24 | 93.3 |
| 25–49 | 91.9 |
| 50–74 | 91.9 |
| 75–99 | 85.1 |
| 100–199 | 96.8 |
| More than 200 | 96.7 |
| All firms | 94.3 |

Source: Wells, "Taxicab Operating."

Profitability depends on three factors: unit costs, unit revenues, and operating efficiency. Consider, for example, cost per vehicle-mile and revenue per paid mile. For a firm to be profitable, it must minimize its cost per vehicle-mile and maximize its revenue per paid mile. However, neither of these actions would produce a profit unless the firm also achieved a sufficiently high ratio of paid miles to total miles. Thus, all three of these measures must be examined.

According to Wells's survey, the firms with the lowest costs per vehicle-mile fall in the ranges of 100 to 199 cabs (27 cents) and 1 to 9 cabs (31 cents). No pattern is evident in comparing profitability. One would expect that firms with longer trip distances would have lower revenues per paid mile because of the higher fares charged for shorter trips. This result appears to be confirmed except for the two categories of the smallest firms and the category of the largest firms. For the smaller firms the fare structures are apparently so low as to counteract any revenue economies produced by short trip length. For the largest firms the opposite is true: the fares are apparently so high that even the longer trip lengths do not decrease the revenues generated per paid mile. Table 8.8 shows these results.

TABLE 8.8. *Revenue and Trip Length*

| Number of Taxis in Fleet | Paid Miles per Trip | Revenue per Paid Mile | Paid Miles as a Percentage of Total Miles |
|---|---|---|---|
| 1–9 | 2.12 | $ .63 | 59 |
| 10–24 | 2.53 | .66 | 56 |
| 25–49 | 2.59 | .84 | 49 |
| 50–74 | 2.86 | .79 | 56 |
| 75–99 | 2.94 | .71 | 59 |
| 100–199 | 2.82 | .70 | 46 |
| More than 200 | 3.02 | .89 | 53 |
| All firms | 2.85 | .83 | 52 |

Source: Wells, "Taxicab Operating."

As seen from Table 8.8, firms in the 75 to 99 cab category do not have the highest revenues, nor do they have the lowest unit costs. But they have the highest profitability because they have the highest ratio of paid to total miles. That is, they are most efficient in their ability to minimize the percentage of deadhead, or nonproductive, miles. The result is that their revenue per vehicle-mile is $.42, compared to a cost of $.34.

## ECONOMIC TRENDS AND THE FUTURE OF THE INDUSTRY

Despite data inadequacies and limitations, it appears certain that taxi firms in the United States are facing difficult times financially. Rapid escalations in costs have forced taxi operators to ask for more frequent fare increases in the ongoing effort to keep up with costs, and taxi passengers, often persons of low income, have had to face paying higher fares. If these trends continue, as some operators expect, the taxi industry will become a service only for the well-to-do. Higher fares will force low-income persons to forego trips or petition governments for publicly subsidized transport services, and local governments will increasingly become a provider of these services. Taxi operators will find their clientele smaller in number and made up to a greater extent of relatively high-income persons. The result will be a smaller taxi industry serving mainly airports and hotels and the virtual elimination of taxis in smaller cities. This scenario might be likened to the fate of the privately owned urban bus firms of the late 1950s.

Whether this scenario will become reality is not, of course, certain. What is certain is that both the industry and public officials can take definite actions to reduce that likelihood. These actions are explored further in later chapters.

# 9

# SERVICE INNOVATIONS

Public transportation at the urban level is not working very well. While the situation is much improved over that of a decade ago, mass transit systems still face massive and growing deficits. Services in suburban areas, cross-town services, and rural and small-city services are generally inadequate or nonexistent. Recent increases in ridership demonstrate the severely limited capacity of many systems to accommodate the shifts to transit that might be produced by an energy emergency. Nor is the taxi industry in a better position. Costs have escalated faster than revenues; diversification has been slow; and fleets are disappearing. In general, taxi firms remain outside of the local public transportation funding process. Despite more than a decade of committed federal transit funding, local public transportation still has many problems.

This situation contrasts with the vision of many transportation professionals of a future in which coordinated urban public transportation services reinforce—and are reinforced by—land-use policies. Many people, particularly transit users, have observed that downtown-focused, radial transit service no longer fits the travel patterns of persons in a sprawling urban region that contains many business, commercial, and cultural centers. There the need is for cross-town services, neighborhood services, and much interaction and coordination between these various services.

In the early 1970s transportation professionals began using the term *paratransit* in describing hopeful solutions to transit problems that required, not highly sophisticated new technology, but a commonsense utilization of existing, rather mundane, and normally overlooked services. The term *paratransit* soon included car pooling, van pooling, taxicabs, dial-a-bus, subscription bus, and even hitchhiking. Paratransit became defined not by the vehicle used but by the type of service provided. Never again could urban transportation services be easily defined; instead terms such as "demand-responsive general service with no advance reservation" became common, and distinctions between terms such as "dial-a-bus" and "shared-ride taxi" became blurred.

At the heart of the enthusiasm for paratransit was the idea that paratransit services could be coordinated with each other and with largely existing services to provide effective service for low-density areas and more cost-efficient service for everyone. This "Paratransit Dream" required no new technology, only the solution of a few management and political problems. Conferences, reports, and books spread the paratransit message. Surely, its proponents felt, knowledge of paratransit would lead local decision makers to coordinate existing services and implement new ones. The dream would become reality.

Yet despite this optimism it remains more vision than reality. As recently as 1979 it was estimated that 308 coordinated paratransit systems were in operation in the United States.[1] While this estimate may not be precise, what is important is that coordinated paratransit systems are still novel enough to be counted. The widespread proliferation of diverse, flexible, imaginative coordinated paratransit services has not happened.

Nonetheless, the dream remains a potent and attractive one. The vision of public and private providers operating in concert and using a variety of types of vehicles promises better and less costly service. The financial problems facing both transit and taxi operators make coordinated paratransit systems doubly attractive. A closer examination of specific paratransit services and some of the hurdles they face in implementation should help give a note of realism to the projections of the visionaries.

## CONVENTIONAL TAXICAB SERVICES

In recent decades the taxicab has primarily provided exclusive-ride service: that is, service in which one party has exclusive use of the vehicle at any one time. As earlier chapters in this volume have shown, however, the early taxicab firms often provided shared-ride service.

Service Innovations / 125

Local ordinances passed to protect the streetcar systems and the widespread use of taximeters combined to shift taxi operations toward exclusive-ride service.

Not surprisingly, taxi operators—and passengers—pay a price for reserving a vehicle for only one party at a time. Although almost all taxis can carry five, and in many cases seven, passengers, most parties consist of only one person; the average number of passengers per trip is only 1.46. In some cities this exclusive use of taxis is called "premium" service, an apt term which distinguishes it from other more productive and lower-cost types of taxi service. Whereas bus and rapid-rail systems collectively carry about 3.6 passengers per vehicle-mile, taxicabs average about 0.28 passengers per vehicle-mile, or 0.54 passengers per paid mile, still much lower than the productivity of bus and rail. The result, of course, is a higher cost per passenger-mile for exclusive-ride service than for shared-ride service. Part of this higher cost is for the extra fuel used. In fact, during the 1979 fuel shortage, New York City authorized shared-riding as a fuel conservation measure. The irony of this action is apparent when one recalls that New York was alone among major cities in refusing to take a similar step during World War II.

Despite the conventional focus on exclusive-ride service, taxi operators have for many years provided a number of other services, the most common of which are shown in Table 9.1. The percentages in the table, however, are deceiving: they do not indicate the extent to which these services are provided. A better indication of diversification is provided by the types of vehicles owned. Wells found that 90 percent of the vehicles owned by taxi firms are taxicabs. While taxi operators have invested in other types of vehicles, such as limousines, minibuses, vehicles for the handicapped, and school buses, none of these vehicle types accounted for more than 1.5 percent of the total number of vehicles owned by taxi operators in 1976.

These statistics, however, are old. Since Wells's 1976 survey the economics of taxi operations have changed substantially, as fuel prices have risen and as many operators have entered into contracts for a variety of publicly funded services. It is likely, therefore, that the current distribution of vehicle types is less heavily skewed toward the taxicab sedan.

TABLE 9.1. *Conventional Taxi Services*

| Service | Percentage of Operations Providing Service |
| --- | --- |
| Package delivery | 71 |
| School children | 44 |
| Company employees | 43 |
| Hospital patients | 31 |
| Handicapped persons | 25 |
| Government employees | 11 |
| Senior citizens / public aid | 10 |
| Blood, hospital supplies | 5 |

Source: Wells, "Taxicab Operating."

## INNOVATIVE TAXICAB SERVICES

Obvious pitfalls await any attempt to describe "innovations" in an area as dynamic as paratransit. What is innovative today will likely become commonplace in the near future, and what is innovative in one city may be already considered conventional in another. Nonetheless, from an industry-wide perspective a number of ideas have only begun to be implemented, and these might therefore be called innovations.

One way to categorize paratransit innovations in taxi operations is to distinguish between innovations pertaining to services, those involving markets served, and those that concern organizational changes. Examples of each of these three categories are shown in Figure 9.1; all of these are currently being implemented by taxi operators in the United States. In general, the market innovations suggest that taxi operators are taking a broader view of potential taxi users, and the organizational innovations suggest that they are gaining a wider perspective on how taxi firms can be managed.

The service innovations, however—the taxi firm's output—are the most important. Taxicab services can be characterized using four criteria: (a) method and amount of payment; (b) type and ownership of vehicle; (c) method of arranging for service; and (d) type of vehicle occupancy. Conventional exclusive-ride taxi service represents only one of many combinations of these factors, namely, a five- or seven-passenger vehicle carrying a single party who has telephoned or hailed the cab and pays the driver upon leaving the cab. Many other

FIGURE 9.1. *Taxi-Operated Paratransit Innovations*

| | |
|---|---|
| Markets | Industrial Supplies<br>Package Delivery<br>Message and mail delivery<br>Door-knob advertising<br>Social service clients<br>School children<br>Exceptional school children<br>Employees on-the-job<br>Elderly |
| Organization | Leasing<br>Association<br>Shared dispatching<br>Satellite taxis<br>In-vehicle telephone dispatching<br>Management information systems |
| Service | Shared-ride or dial-a-ride<br>Jitney or hail-a-ride<br>Plan-a-ride<br>Subscription or pool-a-ride<br>Charter<br>Transit feeder or transfer<br>Fare variations<br>Contract for service<br>Contract for vehicle operation |

combinations are possible, and these combinations represent the wide range of service innovations available to taxi operators.

One way to categorize service innovations is by the markets they serve. Systan, a consulting firm, has distinguished between paratransit services that serve anyone ("general market") and those that serve selected groups ("target market").[2] Multisystems, also a consulting firm, uses a similar approach, defining "general community," "specialized," "work trip," and "rural" services.[3] In both the intent is the same: to differentiate services according to the type of demand they are intended to serve.

### GENERAL MARKET SERVICES

This category includes services that are operated on a shared-ride basis and are available to anyone within a specified service area. These services may be subsidized by a public agency, and if subsidized, the subsidy may go directly to the provider or to the users. As in most paratransit services, the vehicle used may be a sedan, a van, a small bus, or even a large bus. A general market taxi service differs from a dial-a-bus service only in that a private taxi operator, rather than a transit system, operates the service.

Actual examples of general market services exhibit the wide variations which one would expect with such a broad service concept. Some services require advanced reservations; others do not. Some serve only a neighborhood; others serve entire cities. Some operate both night and day; others operate only a few hours per day. These variations are reflected in a study of twenty-eight general market services, the results of which appear in Table 9.2. The wide range in parameters for these twenty-eight examples is generally comparable to the results for fifty dial-a-bus systems surveyed in the same study. This similarity implies that there is more variation between general service taxi systems than between them and dial-a-bus systems.

One relatively common version of this innovation is the taxi-operated dial-a-ride. Both California and Michigan have pioneered in the testing of this concept, particularly in suburban and small-city areas. Some of the California examples are summarized in Table 9.3. Each of these systems was subsidized using a direct provider subsidy:

TABLE 9.2. *Characteristics of Twenty-eight General Market Taxi Systems (1979)*

|  | Median | Range |
|---|---|---|
| Fleet size | 5.8 | 1–75 |
| Fares | $ .50 | $ .15–$1.00 |
| Trips per 1,000 population | 4.3 | 1.0–27.6 |
| Trips per square mile per hour | 1.4 | 0.2–5.0 |
| Trip length (miles) | 2.6 | .8–3.7 |
| Passengers per vehicle-hour | 5.5 | 2.85–8.7 |
| Cost per passenger | $1.70 | $1.05–$2.94 |

Source: Systan, *Paratransit Handbook.*

that is, contracts were executed between the operators and the local municipalities. However, the contracts and the operating arrangements differ. Some cities, such as Barstow, La Mesa, Huntington Park, and Arcadia, paid the taxi operator on a vehicle-mile basis; other contracts were based on per-hour payments. Both of these arrangements are conservative in that the cities limit their expenditures to a fixed amount and the operator prices his services to return a small profit. Since he gives all the fares to the city, any incentive to improve or expand the service is absent, for the operator gains nothing by carrying more passengers. Other cities allow the operator to keep the fares as an incentive to increase ridership.

Not all general market services are publicly subsidized. A number of taxi operators have long provided shared-ride service either as an option or as the only type of service. An example of the latter is Black and White Checker Cab in Little Rock, which has used shared-riding for thirty years. Operating on a zone system, Black and White in 1977 charged $.65 for travel within any one zone and $.35 for each additional zone. A three-mile trip in Little Rock cost approximately $1.70, compared to an average of $2.31 for fifty cities in 1977. The dispatchers asked where a party was, where they wanted to go, and how many persons were in the party. The dispatcher then called for taxis in the area of the pick-up to respond, and one was chosen which was

TABLE 9.3. *Summary of California Paratransit Operations (1976)*

| Location | Contractor | Sponsoring Agency | Population |
|---|---|---|---|
| Los Angeles, Pacoina | Para-Transit Limited | City of Los Angeles | 42,000 |
| Monrovia | San Gabriel Valley Cab | City of Monrovia | 30,000 |
| Ontario | Paul's Yellow Cab | West Valley Transit | 30,000 |
| San Bernadino | San Bernadino Yellow Cab | City of San Bernadino | 35,000 |
| Arcadia | San Gabriel Valley Cab | City of Arcadia | 47,000 |
| Barstow | Barstow Yellow Cab | City of Barstow | 18,500 |
| Claremont | Paul's Yellow Cab | City of Claremont | 25,000 |
| El Cajon | San Diego Yellow Cab | City of El Cajon | 61,500 |
| La Mesa | San Diego Yellow Cab | City of La Mesa | 45,000 |
| Huntington Park | All-American Cab | City of Huntington | 33,000 |
| Los Angeles-Beverly Fairfax | Los Angeles Cab | City of Los Angeles | 75,000 |

Source: International Taxicab Association and personal visits.

| Vehicle Ownership | Monthly Ridership | Fare | Subsidy Per Rider |
|---|---|---|---|
| P-T, Ltd. | 3,400 | .15 | 2.93 |
| San Gabriel Valley Cab | 770 | .75 | 1.10 |
| West Valley Transit | 1,210 | .50 | 2.83 |
| City of San Bernadino | 8,300 | .50 | 1.45 |
| San Gabriel Valley Cab | 4,830 | .75 | 1.06 |
| City of Barstow | 2,300 | .36 | 0.95 |
| Paul's Yellow Cab | 1,826 | .35 | 0.84 |
| San Diego Yellow Cab | 16,800 | .50 | 0.85 |
| City of La Mesa | 8,900 | .50 | 0.93 |
| All-American Cab | 7,500 | .50 | 1.25 |
| Los Angeles Yellow Cab | 6,344 | .15 | 2.05 |

going in the general direction of the trip requested. This "bidding" procedure by drivers worked well except for the times when a driver lied about his location.

The advantage of shared-riding is obvious: greater vehicle productivity and hence lower costs per passenger and lower fares. For example, Black and White Checker averaged about .2 trips per mile for a fourteen-month period during 1974–75. For March 1975 Black and White serviced .216 trips per mile. For the same month, fourteen other exclusive-ride operations in the nation averaged only .172 trips per mile. Wells's study shows that for 667 operations in 1973 the average was about .164 trips per mile.[4]

The Little Rock example demonstrates that a firm can be successful providing shared-ride service without subsidy as its predominant service. The success of this system, however, partly reflects its longevity; Little Rock taxi users have long been accustomed to sharing taxis. Firms that introduce shared-riding face substantial challenges in instructing would-be passengers about how it works and in overcoming their fears of riding in a taxi with strangers. As a result, many operators who have introduced shared-riding have added it as a service option, rather than offer it exclusively.

The concept of service options is a new but important one for taxi operators. In most service industries, including transportation industries, a customer has a choice of levels of service and prices from which to choose. This multiple-product approach allows a firm to meet the needs of more people and marks the firm as a customer-oriented one. In the taxi business, however, normally only one level of service is provided, and the passenger has no options. Even those firms that do offer more than one level of service, say shared-ride and exclusive-ride, seldom market those options.

One exception is Yellow Cab of Stroudsburg, Pennsylvania. In 1963 Yellow Cab began providing shared-ride service in addition to exclusive-ride service. As a response to the 1973–74 oil embargo, the firm added a third service level, "plan-a-ride," in which passengers received substantial fare reductions by requesting service at least two hours in advance. Potential taxi users in Stroudsburg therefore have three levels of service from which to choose, and these options are continually marketed to the public. A person desiring inexpensive transportation can choose the plan-a-ride option and perhaps share the vehicle with another passenger, while a person seeking a quicker trip or unwilling to share a vehicle can elect the exclusive-ride option.

Companies may offer optional fare levels even without providing optional service levels. In many service industries the price charged depends on when the service is rendered. For example, peak-load pricing of electricity offers savings for persons using electricity during low-demand hours. In the taxi industry this concept has been used in the form of surcharges in some cities for nighttime service. In a sense this use of differential pricing is the reverse of peak-load pricing in that it penalizes persons requesting service during off-peak hours.

However, the peak-load concept could be applied to taxi service. In many cities, particularly smaller ones, the issuance of social security and welfare checks at the beginning of each month produces an early-month ridership peak and a late-month ridership decline. Likewise, many firms experience dramatic differences in trips according to the day of the week. In both instances the taxi operator could stimulate demand during slow days by offering lower fares, giving potential customers the option of postponing a shopping trip, for example, and thereby saving money on the taxi fare. The aim of such a program would be a net increase in the total taxi passengers each month, not just a redistribution of trips from early month to late month. In most cities this variation in fares would require local ordinance change. Seattle, for example, has recently adopted a new taxi ordinance which gives the operator the freedom to adopt differential fares.

General market shared-ride taxi service has been implemented in several special situations to provide particular types of service. Each of these situations still qualifies as a general market service in that everyone in the market area is eligible to use the service.

In a transit feeder service shared-ride taxis transport persons to and from transfer points served by fixed-route transit. The major advantage of this service is that it provides access to transit for areas for which fixed-route service would be impractical or prohibitively expensive. In this way transit systems can shorten routes and save money without eliminating service to these low-density areas. Feeder services can also be designed to run only during off-peak hours, supplementing regular transit service during peak hours.

While many of the dial-a-ride systems—those in California, particularly—serve transit transfer points, transit feeder systems are still few in number. In Arabi, Louisiana, a taxi operator, who also owns the local bus company, has set up a taxi-bus transfer system in which buses serve two corridors and the taxis serve the rest of the city. In Petersborough, Ontario, the transit systems suspended service to two outlying suburban areas and contracted with a taxi firm to transport people to and from the transit terminal points. A similar service was recently put into practice in Norfolk by the Tidewater Transit District. In Chapel Hill, North Carolina, off-peak shared-ride service on portions of two routes takes people to transit transfer points. Chapel Hill also uses shared-ride taxis as an evening replacement for its buses.

The limited number of examples of transit feeder systems does not reflect the potential that this idea holds for transit innovations. Rather, the problems posed by section 13c of the Urban Mass Transportation Act, discussed in chapter 7, make it difficult to curtail transit service and contract with private providers. Most of these examples are special instances in which federal operating funds have not been used.

A second special application of general market services is the community or neighborhood circulation service. This application has many forms, ranging from small-town service to service in neighborhoods or suburbs of large cities. Examples include the dial-a-ride systems in Orange County, California, in which local circulation service is provided in addition to service to transit transfer points.

A particularly interesting example is the Michigan program of transit assistance.[5] Funded by state tax revenues, this program provides complete first-year funding and partial funding thereafter for transit services. Initially the program was only for cities with populations under fifty thousand, but later it was expanded to include the entire state. While suburban Detroit areas and rural counties are now included in the program it is the small-city element which is the oldest and in some ways most interesting. In most states small cities have little or no transit service, but the Michigan program has encouraged them to try demand-responsive services. Fully half of these cities have elected to contract with local taxi firms to provide these services. The result has been low-cost service which has strengthened rather than displaced private operators.

These examples by no means exhaust the possible applications of general market services. Taxi pools are taxi-operated versions of van pools and car pools. Route taxis are fixed-route taxicabs used to supplement transit service during times of high demand or to replace it during conditions of very low demand. Jitney taxis, illegal in most American cities, provide fixed-route, nonscheduled service along heavily traveled corridors. All of these examples, rather than delimit the applications of general market service, instead demonstrate the breadth of such applications.

### TARGET MARKET SERVICES

In many instances a transportation service is intended to serve only selected groups of people. For example, because of their special needs, the aged and the handicapped are frequently designated to receive special transportation services. Target market services differ from general market services in that persons must meet some eligibility requirement in order to use the service.

Even though target market services have been in existence for many years, the concept of special services has recently become a matter of philosophical and legal debate. The Rehabilitation Act of 1973 requires facilities and services financed by federal funds to be accessible to handicapped persons, and the Department of Transportation has subsequently required that transit systems be made accessible. The debate over this requirement has centered on the costs of providing such accessibility and on whether special services would better meet the needs of handicapped persons. Opponents of the full accessibility requirement—called the section 504 regulations—maintain that accessibility would serve only a small percentage of the handicapped population, while for much less money cities could operate special, door-to-door services for handicapped persons. Proponents argue that accessibility to public facilities is an inherent right of all citizens.

This debate notwithstanding, special services for target groups will no doubt continue to exist. One reason is that many special services are funded by human service programs. These programs are not only not funded by the Department of Transportation—and not subject to section 504 regulations—but they are also designed to serve special target groups. For example, many programs have been set up to provide nutrition centers for elderly persons, services for disabled persons, medical services for low-income persons, and many more. Most of these have components which provide funding for transportation to and from these services. These programs will continue to provide or contract for target market services, regardless of the section 504 regulations. Moreover, many cities will likely continue to provide special market transit services of various types to handicapped and elderly persons.

Target market services are organized and provided in many different ways. Some agencies operate their own vehicles; others contract for service. Some agencies lease their vehicles to private operators who provide the contracted service; others do not. Some agencies enter into cooperative agreements with other agencies for coordinated service; others act independently. These and other options combine to create a great variety in types of target market services. Two considerations, however, deserve elaboration in this discussion of the taxi industry.

The first of these is funding. Target market services are funded either through provider subsidies or user-side subsidies. A provider subsidy funds an operator directly, and the operator agrees to provide specified services. Transit systems receive provider subsidies. A user-side subsidy, on the other hand, may require no contract or agreement with a provider. Instead, users receive money, tokens, vouchers, or tickets to use for existing services.

The user-side subsidy has many advantages for target market services. Eligible persons can be given some form of currency which transportation providers will agree to honor. Persons not in the target group do not receive this currency and hence cannot receive the service. It is, therefore, a simple and direct way to assist specific persons. It also requires no elaborate bidding and contracting process to select providers. Any operator may participate in the program simply by agreeing to accept the currency used.

Taxi firms are currently participating in countless user-side subsidy programs. One simple example familiar to almost all taxi firms is the agreement to transport clients of social service agencies and to bill the agency for the trip costs. In such cases the "currency" is merely a promise by the agency to pay for the trip. Other examples are more formal. Oak Ridge, Tennessee, established a program to serve elderly persons by subsidizing their taxi trips. Eligible persons purchased one-dollar coupons for twenty-five cents, with sixty-five cents paid by the city and ten cents paid by the taxi company. Each coupon is redeemable for one dollar's worth of taxi service.

Many other examples of similar arrangements exist, including four demonstration projects funded by the Urban Mass Transportation Administration. These four are summarized in Table 9.4. All these demonstration projects utilize taxi firms as providers. In each case two or more firms participate, meaning that all firms have an opportunity to compete for the business resulting from the subsidy programs. Thus the user-side subsidy has not restructured the local taxi industry by selecting one firm from among several local firms.

A second basic dimension of target market services is whether the funding agency chooses to provide its own service. Many agencies have done so, and this has meant serious economic harm for taxi operators throughout the country. In recent years careful studies have shown that agency-operated transportation services are normally more expensive than the agency realizes, for they sometimes fail to take into account such costs as administrative time, maintenance, and depreciation. Moreover, the realization that many agency-operated services duplicate existing services has prompted several states to push for coordination of these services.

Taxicab operators have sought a central role in the coordination of such programs. Individual firms have participated in many local efforts to coordinate human service transportation. In some instances, taxi firms merely provide maintenance for agency vans. In many other cases they operate the vans for the agency. In still other instances taxi firms use their own vehicles and provide coordinated services for many different human service agencies. On a larger scale, Allegheny County, Pennsylvania, has implemented a brokerage system in which taxicab firms bid on and receive contracts for human service transportation.

Target market services are vital to the economic health of the taxi industry. The extent to which taxi operators are able to participate in

TABLE 9.4. *User-Side Subsidy Examples*

| Characteristic | Danville, Ill. | Montgomery, Ala. | Kinston, N.C. | Lawrence, Mass. |
|---|---|---|---|---|
| Population | 42,600 | 133,400 | 22,300 | 66,900 |
| Number of taxi firms | 2 | 3 | 8 | 8 |
| Number of taxicabs | 24 | 47 | 33 | 63 |
| Fare discount (percentage) | 50 | 50 | 50 | 50 |
| Subsidy mechanism | Voucher | Voucher | Ticket | Ticket |
| Fare structure | Zone | Zone | Zone | Zone |

Source: Kendall, "Comparison of Findings."

these many programs will continue to be important in determining whether taxi operations will continue to shrink and be supplanted by publicly subsidized services.

## INNOVATION, DIVERSIFICATION, AND SURVIVAL

Much has happened to the taxicab industry since the days when John Hertz cut fares, improved service, and installed traffic lights in Chicago. In those days the taxi industry was an innovative, progressive, market-oriented service industry. Taxi wars and the subsequent regulation of the industry changed all that, but as long as costs were relatively stable and little public money went into local transportation, taxi operations remained profitable undertakings.

Those days, however, have passed. Taxi operators now face severe increases in the costs of fuel, parts, and insurance. They also operate in an environment that is strongly affected by the expenditure of public funds. As a result operators must spend more of their time dealing with public agencies at the local, state, and federal levels, and, according to the Wells surveys, they are finding their profits dwindling and disappearing.

One response to this new operating environment is to change one's methods of operation, and changes are occurring within the industry. Leasing is one example; contracting with public agencies is another. Yet these changes are slow in coming in comparison with the growth of the problems facing the industry. As this chapter has shown, innovative service ideas exist and have been tested. Why, then, is there not more experimentation and innovation at the local level? What happened to the Paratransit Dream in which many varieties of services were to blossom in a flexible, imaginative, yet coordinated fashion?

There are many answers to these questions, some of which have to do with the role of the taxi industry, while others are more general. Taxi operators have in many instances been slow to adapt to their new operating environments which require them to interact with many public agencies. No doubt the image of the industry, an image tarnished by events of several decades ago, continues to haunt taxi operators by making public officials wary of contracting with taxi firms. Change and innovation depend mostly, however, on new ideas and energy, both of which are provided by new people entering the industry. While no data are available on this vital topic, it is safe to surmise that few new people are entering any industry with financial and image problems like those of the taxi industry. The industry is caught in a dilemma: just when it most needs new talent and energy, it most lacks the resources to attract new people.

The slow rate of innovation in and implementation of paratransit programs is not, however, attributable only to the taxi industry. Public officials and transit operators must share the blame. At the local level public officials have been slow to understand the problems facing taxi operators and have done little to update taxi ordinances or to stimulate taxi operators to try new ideas. When such actions have been taken, they have too often been focused on open entry rather than on the real problems of the industry. At the federal level the lack of a policy on UMTA funding of taxis remains a roadblock. The industry has had to expend time and money to achieve and maintain the federal gas tax rebate scheme and to fight harmful legislation, rather than respond to more positive federal initiatives designed to foster and fund innovative services. The transit industry has scarcely been a positive influence. While individual transit operators have made strong efforts to involve taxi operators in their programs, the transit industry as a whole has not. Problems of labor agreements and limited funds have, understandably, made transit operators reluctant to try experimental taxi-operated services. However, the overall lack of communication between the industries at both the national and local levels is not understandable.

While these and other reasons may explain the slowness with which the taxi industry has diversified, they do not diminish the need for such innovation. The survival of the taxi industry depends in no small way on how successful it is in implementing service innovations such as those discussed in this chapter.

# 10

## REGULATION AND DEREGULATION

With the exception of a few brief periods, public concern has seldom focused on the regulation of taxicabs. Indeed, under most conditions, taxicab regulations have rarely seemed an item of much importance. As noted in chapter 3, current taxicab ordinances are but a step in the long evolution of paratransit regulations dating from 1654 in England. Moreover, taxi regulation in the United States is a local responsibility and hence has seldom attracted national attention.

There have been at least two exceptions to this public indifference. One was the Depression, and the other was the period immediately after World War II. These two periods were times of extraordinary economic changes. The taxicab industry in both instances was severely effected by the influx of new owner-operators; the result was chaos and conflict within the industry and irresponsible service to the public. The response from public officials was to enact regulations limiting the number of taxicabs, fixing fares, and specifying allowable services. Advocates of taxicab regulation have often cited the Depression-produced problems as a reason to continue limits on the number of taxicabs. This and other arguments for such regulation will be examined later in this chapter.

It could be argued that the late 1970s began another period of public interest in taxicab regulations. Seattle, Miami, San Diego, and Portland all enacted major changes in their taxicab ordinances. Several state conferences and a national conference on regulatory revision for taxicabs in Kansas City in May 1980 all focused attention on the subject of taxi ordinances.

While certainly less crisis oriented than that during the Depression or postwar periods, this interest is somewhat similar to that of those periods in that it resulted from abnormal economic conditions. Rising energy costs and high inflation created frequent requests from taxi operators for fare increases. In most cities, fare increases meant substantial city staff work to examine the economic necessity for increasing the fares, a task which often included intensive study and auditing of the financial records of the local taxi firms. Thus, more frequent fare increases meant more time spent by city staff and elected officials on taxicab matters. At the same time, the early results of the so-called deregulation of the airlines were focusing public attention on the basic question of whether regulation of transportation was even desirable. Together, these two factors caused local officials to wonder whether the trouble of taxicab regulation was justified.

Ironically, this interest in taxicab regulation had long been sought by taxi operators—but for very different reasons. By the 1970s, taxicab regulations were very much out of date. In fact, a 1978 survey of taxi ordinances in North Carolina found that the average length of time since the last major revision was twenty-three years.[1] Ordinances were found to have negative perspectives and were often punitive. Shared-ride and contract services were often disallowed, and taxi drivers were required to submit to fingerprinting, venereal disease checks, and a variety of "nuisance" provisions. Unfortunately, the North Carolina ordinances are little different from ordinances elsewhere; a public which wants courteous, professional taxi drivers still often has ordinances which treat taxi drivers as criminals.

Thus, while taxi regulation has emerged as a public concern, there is wide disagreement regarding why it is a problem. Some public officials question the need for entry controls and rate setting. Many operators want ordinances to be updated to allow them to implement new services. What is clear is that after two or three decades of neglect, taxi regulation is again receiving public attention.

### CURRENT TAXICAB REGULATIONS

In all but a few states taxicabs are regulated by municipalities.[2] Some limited state regulation occurs in enabling legislation giving municipalities the right to regulate taxicabs. State laws may define the term *taxicab* and may set minimum limits on insurance coverage. Most aspects of taxicab regulation, however, are left to the discretion of local governments.

Among the most common provisions in the taxi ordinances are those which define a "taxicab"; prescribe financial and insurance responsibilities; detail the number of taxi permits allowed and the procedure for issuing permits; prescribe driver licensing procedures; delimit services provided by taxicabs; and set the fares and method of computing fares. Various other provisions are also frequently included. Some of these define the record-keeping responsibilities of operators, require vehicle inspections and the use of meters, and provide for fines and hearings for failing to adhere to the ordinance. Another category includes the "nuisance" provisions that are frequently found in ordinances: prohibiting drivers from spitting; forbidding members of the opposite sex to ride in the front seat with the driver; requiring drivers to be licensed by the police; and prohibiting cruising.

The variety of possible ordinances can be appreciated by considering only the two most controversial provisions of taxi ordinances: fares and entry restrictions. Fares may or may not be computed using taximeters; cities requiring taximeters may also allow nonmeter fares for special services, such as contracts with agencies, airport services, downtown circulation services, or shared-riding. Fares may be specified by ordinance, or maximum fares may be specified. Regardless of the method of computing fares, ordinances commonly specify how the fare levels are to be advertised on both the insides and the outsides of the cabs.

Entry restrictions may also vary widely. Washington, Seattle, and San Diego place no limits on the number of taxis to be licensed. In addition, many smaller cities have no entry restrictions. On the other hand, New York, Boston, and Chicago have limited numbers of medallions, the metal licenses affixed to the hoods of taxicabs. Most other larger cities limit the number of taxis, although not all in the same way. One way is to set a ceiling on the number of licenses; another is to establish a population-to-taxicab license ratio. Still another common way is to require the municipal government to determine whether public convenience and necessity require additional taxicab licenses. Another method is to require firms to have a minimum number of taxis; Portland, Oregon, requires a firm to have fifteen taxis. Still another approach is to grant franchises to firms, with each firm allowed to determine the number of taxis it will operate.

Given these many possibilities, it is understandable why taxi ordinances vary so much from city to city. Ordinances may likewise vary enormously in size. There is no one superior or "model" ordinance; local concerns and conditions influence the approach taken in taxi regulation.

There are, however, some common points of confusion inherent in most ordinances. The first concerns items *not* included in the ordinance. If an ordinance does not mention shared-ride service, it can be interpreted by some municipalities that shared-riding is illegal. The same problem applies to ordinances that do not mention contract services. One city recently spent one year adding eight pages to its ordinance allowing contract services and specifying grievance procedures for taxi firms not selected in a bidding process. The reason for this change was a local interpretation that since the ordinance had not specifically mentioned contract services, they must be illegal.

An equally important ambiguity results from jurisdictional uncertainties. Since cities cannot regulate taxis outside the city limits, taxis are usually self-regulated in nonurban areas. In metropolitan regions this problem is compounded by the existence of many municipal jurisdictions. In such cases a taxi operator may have to seek fare increases from many different local governments. Airports often have regulatory powers and may limit the number of taxis allowed to pick up passengers. The result is confusion and duplication of regulatory efforts.

Another problem common to most regulations is that they seldom provide incentives for operator-initiated service innovations. Many operators, as a result, view the ordinance revision process as so cumbersome that ideas for new services are postponed indefinitely. Finally, without adequate enforcement, the best taxi ordinance is of little value. Yet, little research attention has been given to the time and monetary costs involved in enforcing various ordinance provisions.

The problems of enforcement can be illustrated by considering two examples. Indianapolis opened entry to the local taxi industry by establishing two times, in 1973 and 1974, when anyone could apply for and receive a taxi permit. The result was enormous confusion, as taxis of a rainbow of colors appeared. Many independent owner-operators maintained no office, phone, or address, and passenger complaints were unresolvable because, in many cases, operators could not be located. While this experience does not prove that open entry is unworkable, it does point to the need to consider how enforcement problems can be magnified by precipitous deregulation.

In both San Diego and Seattle restrictions on the numbers of taxi permits were rescinded in 1979. The cities have not deregulated in the true sense of the word; both cities still impose safety, insurance, and financial responsibility requirements. While this approach eliminates the city role in determining the need for additional taxis, it transfers certain responsibilities to other agencies. The airports must now contend with queues of taxis with different rates, since taxis in both cities are allowed to set their own rates. Time previously spent by city staff is now transferred to airport personnel. Also, city staff that previously considered industry petitions for fare increases must spend more time administering the safety and insurance provisions that apply to what is now a larger number of independent taxi firms. It is not known whether the taxi ordinance changes in these two cities have in fact lessened the regulatory burden.

## THE RATIONALE FOR DEREGULATION

Among the many elements of taxicab regulations are two which stand alone because of their controversial nature: entry restrictions and rate limitations. While other regulations, such as safety, insurance, and service quality, are at times subjects of debate regarding how they should be implemented, the fact that they are necessary is seldom questioned. This is not so with respect to entry and fare controls. Many people continually question the need for such controls. Indeed, some smaller cities have no such controls.

There are two principal bases for eliminating fare and entry controls. One is founded on economic theory of pure competition. Simply stated, economic theory holds that under conditions of perfect competition prices and outputs will be determined so that benefits to society as a whole will be maximized. Put another way, unfettered competition in a perfect market will lead to the most efficient allocation of resources. Applied to the taxi industry, this theory has a powerful intuitive appeal. Not the least of its attractive features is its simplicity. Taxi firms should be neither restricted with respect to the fares they charge nor limited in number. Competition, rather than governmental agencies, would dictate price, number of taxis, and surviving and failing firms. The resulting conditions of supply and price would be the most efficient allocation of taxi vehicles, fuel, and drivers.

Proponents of free competition in the taxi industry point to the medallion prices in a few large cities as evidence of waste resulting from entry and fare controls. New York City is the most frequently cited example. Since 1937 New York has limited the number of licensed cabs by requiring medallions. According to economic theory, such supply limitations—if severe enough—will increase profits and affix an economic value to the right to enter the market. One would expect, therefore, that if the limitation on the number of taxi medallions is binding, then the price of a medallion should be substantial, thereby necessitating higher fares in order to generate enough revenues to cover the medallion price. In New York this situation has occurred; the price of a medallion has fluctuated between $5,000 and $68,000 during the last three decades.[3] In Boston medallion prices are also substantial, yet lower than those in New York. In many cities in which entry is limited, however, the price of a license or medallion is undetermined, either because the price is very low or because medallions cannot be traded individually. Despite its publicity, the New York taxicab medallion price remains atypical. It has, nonetheless, been a persuasive factor in bolstering the arguments of those favoring free competition in the taxi industry.

The practical reason for taxicab deregulation is that regulatory agencies must spend much time deciding on rate requests and allocating taxi licenses. Some regulatory agencies have responded to this cost by limiting the number of firms and thereby limiting the number of requests to adjudicate. In other instances, such as the recent regulatory revisions in San Diego and Seattle, the response has been to attempt to remove from public agencies the burden of regulation.

The rationale behind this approach is that since regulation is a time-consuming yet imperfect chore, why not eliminate it. The question that this approach raises is whether a city would be merely transferring to another sector of society, say to an airport authority or consumers, the problems that had previously fallen upon the regulatory agency.

These two rationales—the theoretical and practical—are by no means unrelated. In fact, proponents of open entry and fare competition often cite both reasons. Slogans such as "Get the city out of the taxi business" have an intuitively appealing ring, however superficial the sentiment. Yet politically attractive phrases neither prove nor disprove the economic logic behind deregulation proposals. The validity of such proposals can be ascertained only by examining the soundness of the assumptions of pure competition and perfect markets as they apply to the taxi industry.

## REASONS FOR REGULATION

Taxi ordinances limiting entry and fares have historically resulted from times of market instability. While hackneys and other taxicab ancestors were limited in number and fares charged since 1654, it was the Depression which spurred the regulation of taxis in United States cities. As described in chapter 5, taxis increased dramatically in number during the Depression, and fares declined far below operating costs. The result was chaos, violence, and widespread pleas for restrictions on fares, service quality, and licenses. At first glance it would seem that the free market was not a good allocator of taxicab services.

In his classic work on economic regulation, Alfred Kahn cites many reasons why free competition might not work well in a given industry.[4] Some of these are the result of market imperfections. For example, some industries comprise natural monopolies, for which one characteristic is ever-decreasing average unit costs. For such industries, consumers will experience lower costs if all consumers purchase from a single firm, providing, of course, that regulations prohibit the firm from raising prices to monopoly profit levels. In such industries, competition will lead to duplication of services and production facilities and higher prices to consumers. Implicit subsidies to some competitors induce other market imperfections. For example, railroads, which must pay for the installation and maintenance of trackage, compete with waterway users who have historically paid nothing for the use of federally maintained waterways. Markets may also be imperfect because of important externalities; national defense, for example, warrants the maintenance during peacetime of shipyards that may only be needed during wars. Other market imperfections include the need to assure innovators that they can recoup costs of research and development and the inability of potential customers to evaluate alternative products and services.

There may also be noneconomic reasons for not relying on free competition to allocate resources. Many public utilities require infrastructures that can be built only if eminent domain powers are used; in such cases competition would lead to the wasteful and politically infeasible proliferation of the use of eminent domain. Furthermore, public policy might dictate the internal cross-subsidy of one group, say, rural electricity users, by another, say, urban users. In such a case pure competition would mean either that persons in rural areas would pay much higher prices for electricity or would have no electrical service. Other noneconomic reasons for restricting competition also exist.

The question is: Do any of these reasons, either economic or noneconomic, apply to the taxi industry, and if they do, are they of sufficient importance to warrant restriction of competition? This test is a severe one, for regulation is a costly and imperfect alternative. As Kahn argues, competition should be restricted only in cases in which the disadvantages of free competition clearly outweigh the costs of regulation.

## RUINOUS COMPETITION AND NATURAL MONOPOLY

The chaos within the taxi industry during the Depression was similar to that that occurred within the trucking industry during the same period. The number of owner-operated trucks grew enormously, rates plummetted, and the industry was in turmoil. To ease the situation Congress passed the Motor Carrier Act of 1935, which restricted entry and controlled rates.

This situation has frequently been cited as an example of "ruinous competition," but such was not the case. Ruinous competition occurs when the ratio of fixed to variable costs is high and when an industry has excess capacity for long periods because of losses in business. At such times firms acting independently may lower prices below costs for sustained periods in hopes of increasing sales. In the process a firm may cut costs by compromising standards of quality and safety. If the price cutting continues long enough, firms may be forced out of the market and capacity needed later will have been lost. However, these characteristics—particularly the high ratio of fixed to variable costs—do not fit the trucking industry of the 1930s. It is likely that had the Motor Carrier Act not been passed, the trucking industry would have stabilized, as owner-operators would have left the industry to seek better economic conditions elsewhere.

Like the trucking industry, the taxicab industry apparently experienced the symptoms of ruinous competition, but the classical causes of such competition were not present there either. The taxi industry has a relatively low fixed-to-variable-cost ratio, and excess capacity was the result not only of existing firms losing business but of the entrance of many new owner-operators into the industry. These new owner-operators, who had no other employment, were given the use of unsellable cars on a daily rental basis by manufacturers who were desperate to recoup manufacturing costs. For such owner-operators the taxi business—as bad as it was—was preferable to having no job and no income. Clark has maintained that during times of depression the labor supply increases in the self-employment sector, reflecting the lack of alternative sources of income.[5] This is a better hypothesis to explain the problems that the taxi industry encountered during the early Depression years.

Ruinous competition was not, therefore, the cause of the chaos in the taxi industry during the Depression. It follows that the curtailment of free competition that resulted cannot be justified on the grounds of ruinous competition. It does not follow, however, that entry and price controls are not justified on other economic—or noneconomic—grounds.

One frequently cited market imperfection is natural monopoly. The prerequisite for a natural monopoly is that economies of scale, and, hence, decreasing average costs, occur for all output levels. Often, but not always, this condition occurs when there is a need for large initial investments in productive capacity, such as in the construction of a railroad. In these industries consumers are best served by the monopoly firm as long as regulatory controls prevent predatory pricing by the firm.

The taxi industry has some of the earmarks of a natural monopoly. For smaller firms, say fewer than twenty to thirty vehicles, there are likely to be no appreciable scale economies with respect to costs alone. With the exception of the very smallest firms, all these firms can purchase gasoline in bulk and invest in radio dispatching equipment. Larger firms may be able to achieve some scale economies by computerizing record keeping and developing more extensive in-house maintenance capabilities. Yet even these economies are likely to be small.

When revenue, and hence profit, is considered, however, it appears that larger firms do have access to significant economies of scale. First, they are more likely to be able to respond quickly to trip requests than are many small firms serving the same area independent of each other. Thus, a consumer requesting a taxi by telephone would probably suppose that a large firm would be more likely to have a taxi in his or her vicinity than would a small firm. Small firms sharing dispatching through an association, however, could overcome this disadvantage. Second, larger firms are better able to enter into contracts with public agencies because they often have full-time managers and computerized bookkeeping. Since such contracts are an increasingly important source of funds and can provide revenues during off-peak times, this advantage is an important one.

So the taxi industry is not a natural monopoly. From a profit standpoint, however, firms larger than some medium level are likely to be able to generate greater revenues per hour as their size increases. This is not to say, however, that a monopoly exists if new firms can always enter the market and compete at airports and hotels where demand is high and the larger firm has no inherent advantage. The continued infusion of such new firms may prevent any firm from reaching such a size as to enjoy appreciable returns to scale on the demand side. In such instances the taxi industry will be marked by many smaller firms, none of which will likely devote resources to innovative services, equipment, or management.

Applying Kahn's rule of regulating competition only when there is a clear need to do so, the monopoly argument may or may not justify regulation. If a city is content with many smaller firms, the monopoly rationale does not apply. If a city desires a more innovative industry, however, particularly one with which contracts for joint transit-paratransit services can be more easily let, then having one or a few larger firms is advantageous.

## OTHER MARKET IMPERFECTIONS

Several other reasons why a market may not function perfectly are applicable to taxicab services. Some of these will become apparent upon consideration of a few idiosyncrasies of the taxi market.

Customers can purchase taxi services in two ways: either by hailing a passing vehicle or by some sort of advance reservation, usually by telephone. Actually some of the telephone requests approximate a street hail in that a person wants immediate service. It is not certain, therefore, that a "market" in the pure economic sense even exists. At issue is whether a customer can and does shop among various taxi firms and select the "best" one. For example, even if regulation set fares for all taxis, a customer might select the firm that could respond most quickly to his trip request. For persons planning in advance, such "shopping" could occur. However, for persons hailing a taxi or telephoning for immediate service such shopping is impractical.

Shopping may be possible in a few special cases, and its advocates often cite airport queues and hotel cab stands as examples, urging that if the cabs varied in price and quality, a person could select the "best" one. A number of practical problems render this sort of shopping impossible in most instances. First, space on airport or hotel stands is usually severely limited and cabs not at the head of the line often do not have a safe manner in which to pull out from the queue when hired. Second, there is no way in which one cab can be made to wait while a prospective passenger goes shopping. Third, almost every community has a regulation forbidding cab drivers from refusing service to prospective passengers on the grounds that the driver does not like the trip or the passengers, but if the passengers can shop, it is difficult to prevent the drivers from shopping also. Consequently, most large airports have elaborate systems of taxi queues so that drivers receive trips on a first-in-first-out basis, irrespective of whether a passenger wants to go one block or twenty miles. Customer "shopping" undermines this system and creates problems for airport officials in ensuring order among drivers.

Moreover, it is highly unlikely that a customer could accurately shop for the least expensive taxi even in the special case of a taxi queue that remained stable long enough for him or her to compare fares. Since fares can be expressed in different fractions of a mile and different drop charges and waiting time charges, a passenger would not be able to compute his fare, since he would not know in advance the distance or the time that his trip would take. This situation occurred in Seattle after the deregulation of taxi fares there; operators chose a variety of fares expressed in various fractions of a mile and drop charges. Along with the different waiting time charges used, these different rate structures rendered comparative shopping nearly impossible. To make comparative shopping reasonably practical, regulations would have to specify how each taxi could express its fares; for example, each taxi might be required to compute mileage charges per tenths of a mile.

A market for at least some taxi services could exist if firms were to differentiate their services by advertising. For example, a firm could advertise lower fares than competing firms or guarantee pick-up within, say, fifteen minutes of a telephone request. A person hailing a cab could wait to hail a cab from a particular firm. However, these situations have occurred rarely, even considering only cities which are not regulated. In addition, this "market" does not protect the out-of-town visitor or the person who must travel late at night, when taxi competition may not exist.

A second possible imperfection is commonly called "cream skimming." This problem arises when profits from one part of a business are used to subsidize parts of a business that lose money; the cream skimming occurs when competitors siphon off only the lucrative business. This situation is most often alleged to occur when a common carrier is forced to serve low-density areas or nonpeak times, but faces competition, legal or otherwise, during peak times and in high-volume areas. This has been a familiar charge within the taxi industry. Firms licensed to serve a city face many constraints which encourage internal subsidies. A firm may be required by local ordinance to provide twenty-four-hour service. State and federal laws require a driver to make a minimum wage, meaning that off-peak drivers may have to be subsidized by peak-hour profits. In every city firms are required to serve all requests within their service areas, meaning that persons in low-density areas are often subsidized by persons in high-volume areas. When gypsy, or unlicensed, taxis siphon business and profits from the lucrative airport, hotel, and other high-volume business, they severely limit the profits that licensed carriers need to sustain other required services. The possibility of opening entry to a taxi market also raises fears that newcomers would focus on these more lucrative areas, and experience in some cities has validated these fears.

Many economists argue that the problem is not competition but rather regulation. Free competition would drive down the costs of taxi fares in high-volume business segments, but drastically raise fares for low-density areas or night service. In fact, these fares might go so high that demand would disappear and firms would leave that portion of the market. Since local governments usually desire taxi service for such nonprofitable market segments, public subsidies could be used to maintain such services. Thus, taxes rather than regulation would fund services considered necessary.

The issue of regulation versus subsidy goes beyond economic principles. While it may be more efficient economically to use subsidies, other concerns, such as equity and political acceptability, intervene. The choice, however, underscores the fundamental fact that free competition alone will not result in taxi service for everyone.

A third possible market imperfection clearly applies to taxicab services. For many goods and services there is a certain value in having them available even if they are not used. In some cases this value accrues to nonusers. Many nonusers of taxicabs are comforted in knowing that taxicabs exist in case they might someday need one. Nonresidents know that taxis are available when they visit a city. Indeed, many conventions and trade shows ascertain the availability of adequate taxi service before committing themselves to a particular city. Moreover, hotels, restaurants, sports arenas, and similar places benefit directly from the existence of taxi service. These values are not priceable, and they cannot be reflected in the fares that users pay. Free competition among users would not take these values into account, though if free competition resulted in the discontinuation of taxi services, such benefits would be lost. Again, subsidies are one way of reflecting these values and maintaining service. In the case of public transit, a service with similar external values, subsidies have been granted, in part, for just such reasons.

Among the many other possible market imperfections is one which looms large within the taxi industry. Free competition within the taxi industry makes sense only if free competition exists among urban travel alternatives in general. Taxis do not compete only with each other; they compete with various transit services and with automobiles. Neither of these alternatives exists in a situation of unfettered competition. The automobile is subsidized by the use of nonfuel taxes for street construction and right-of-way acquisition, as well as the unpriced costs to society of such things as pollution, noise, and sprawling development. Transit is heavily subsidized, and these subsidized programs include some demand-responsive systems that are very similar to taxi services. If all urban transit modes were subject to free competition, a stronger case could be made for open entry within the taxi industry.

## NONECONOMIC CONSIDERATIONS

There is one noneconomic reason for restricting competition within the taxi industry. The development of innovative transit services requires ingenuity, energy, capital, and management expertise from the private sector as well as the public sector. Taxi feeder systems, peak-hour supplemental services, low-density transit replacement services, and others all require the cooperation of talented managers in the private sector with public transit authorities. To the extent that the taxi industry is fragmented, firms will be unable to develop individuals with these attributes. Simply put, innovation in local transportation depends, in part, on the development of larger, economically healthy taxi firms that have the management expertise and capital necessary for experimental services.

## OPEN ENTRY VERSUS REGULATORY REVISION

This chapter has dealt in great detail with taxi regulation and the reasons for and against restricting competition within the industry. In one sense this focus on entry and price controls is justified by the controversy that these subjects elicit in many cities. The questions of proper fare levels and who should have licenses are difficult local decisions. The reasoning in this chapter leads to the conclusion that, although difficult, such decisions must be made, for a variety of reasons.

Entry and fare controls are not the only regulations that deserve attention. In fact, taxi ordinances in general are woefully archaic and in need of substantial revisions. Many ordinances predate subsidized urban transit, energy shortages, human services transportation, large, multijurisdictional urban areas, and many other changes. They reflect a different time with different problems. There is, therefore, a need for regulatory revision rather than deregulation.

Regulatory reform should concentrate on ordinances that would protect the public yet still allow for much-needed innovation. Firms could be permitted to offer a variety of services at different levels of fare. Nonmeter fares could be allowed. The taxi firm—not the police—could be held accountable for a driver's conduct and appearance. Shared-riding could be made legal. Nuisance provisions could be removed.

Such positive ordinances have been the goal of recent regulatory changes in several cities. More changes, however, are necessary before taxi ordinances can become an incentive for innovation rather than a barrier to it, and before these changes can occur, local officials must look beyond entry and fare controls and focus on the real problems with local taxi ordinances.

# 11

## DIMENSIONS OF CHANGE

Something happened to the taxicab industry during the 1970s. As public policy focused on reviving public transit and meeting the mobility needs of the elderly, the handicapped, and the poor, the taxicab industry was undergoing a fundamental change. Although the industry remained in private hands and did not receive federal subsidies, it did move quietly through the back door into the public sector.

The ramifications of this shift have yet to be completely understood, but the emergence of publicly funded competitors can be understood easily enough. The rise in government expenditures for public transit was detailed in chapter 7, and over one-half billion dollars in federal monies is spent each year on a plethora of transportation programs run by human service agencies. While the economic effects of this competition from the public sector are acutely felt by taxi operators, the other effects of these governmental programs are not limited to the stimulation of new competition. A fundamental change has occurred in the environment in which taxi firms operate; public agencies, rather than individuals, have become important if not dominant consumers of local transportation services.

For the operator this change means increased costs. A taxi operator who seeks to do business with a transit authority, a human service agency, or a local or state government must be willing to attend meetings, keep extensive data, enter into formal contracts, respond to requests for proposals, tolerate delays in receiving payments, and perhaps be subject to political events which cancel contracts.

The increase in public funds for local transportation has also affected public policy regarding the taxi industry. Until the 1970s there was no need for federal policymakers to direct their attention to the taxi industry. Taxis were a local concern, and one could safely argue that except in times of war or fuel shortage federal actions did little to affect the taxi industry directly. The large federal role in funding local transportation services, however, changed this situation. Suddenly it mattered very much to taxi operators how the federal government chose to spend its transportation funds at the local level. This change has become so complete that policies of such diverse agencies as the National Labor Relations Board, the Internal Revenue Service, the Urban Mass Transportation Administration, the Department of Health and Human Services, and a host of other federal agencies directly affect not only the financial health of the taxi industry but also how the industry is organized and managed. No longer is the relevance of federal policies regarding taxis a debatable issue; even the absence of formal policies is in itself an important policy.

Changing economic conditions within the industry as well as changes in the programs and policies of the public sector create stimuli to which taxi operators must respond. Understanding these changes and what they mean for the future of the taxi industry is a complex task.

## PUBLIC SECTOR ACTIONS AFFECTING TAXI OPERATORS

The many agencies at the different levels of government make what amount to countless decisions which affect the taxi industry. Yet among these decisions a few stand out as more significant, and it is these programs and policies which must be understood and monitored if one is to understand what the taxi industry is likely to be in the future.

### TAXI-TRANSIT INTEGRATION

In 1978 the transit systems of the United States provided approximately 7,616 million revenue-paying trips. This figure is 45 percent higher than the all-time low ridership of 1972. It is also 35 percent above the 1975 ridership, which averaged 36.4 trips per resident of metropolitan areas. Unfortunately, the transit systems recorded an unprecedented deficit of $2.33 billion. For each transit ride in 1978 the transit industry lost 30.6 cents.

158 / The Taxicab

The rising transit deficit, coupled with the increasing public subsidy of transit, has produced a number of problems. One is that the public now views transit service as a public service rather than as a business, which makes it politically difficult to provide transit service in some areas of a city but not in others. Local governments usually choose to maintain marginal transit service in low-density areas so as to avoid political difficulties. A second problem is more than a bit ironical. The demise of transit has been accompanied by a shrinkage in the supply of transit vehicles. Currently, only two United States manufacturers make full-size buses, and during the late 1970s federal policies regarding implementing new design standards for a proposed standardized bus hampered production. As a result, the capacities of the nation's transit systems are strained. A 1979 survey of transit systems found that 34 percent of the nation's transit systems could not accommodate even a 30 percent increase in ridership.[1] Yet, if as few as 10 percent of those who now commute by automobile were to switch to transit—a not unrealistic figure in another energy crisis—transit ridership would approximately double. Transit systems are in the unfortunate position of not being able to withstand even a modest, short-term switch of automobile users.

Taxicabs, and paratransit in general, provide a means to alleviate some of these financial and operating problems facing transit. Shared-ride taxi service can serve low-density suburban areas and provide feeder service to transit lines. Taxis can be used to replace transit service during low-density times of the day, and they can decrease the need for peak-hour buses by supplementing transit service during times of peak demand. These and other service innovations have been described in chapter 9.

The inclusion of taxi services within mass transit services implies a substantial change in the manner in which transit services are operated. One such change would reduce the size and scale of the services provided by metropolitan transit authorities. For example, a transit authority might be responsible only for buses or rail vehicles that run along designated heavy-demand corridors. Service in areas outside these corridors could be provided by many private operators, including taxi operators, using vans, sedans, and buses. A public agency would monitor the quality of these various services and serve as a broker to determine which operators would serve which areas. At the heart of this approach is the assumption that large transit authorities have no inherent economies of scale and hence cannot provide region-wide service more cheaply than could many smaller operators.

A second way to include taxi-operated services is to create public transit authorities that would bring taxi services under their umbrella. Some authorities have already contracted with taxi operators and implemented paratransit services to augment or replace fixed-route transit services. This arrangement is hampered by the section 13c labor provision, discussed in chapter 9, which makes it difficult for federal funds to be used for services that would reduce the need for transit labor and thus reduce labor costs.

Regardless of how paratransit services are integrated with transit services, taxi-operated services have shown themselves to be more cost-effective than similar services provided by transit authorities, even in cases in which taxi operators use vans or small buses that are identical to those used by transit operators. The reasons they have been able to do so lie in the cost structure and management of taxi firms. Taxi labor is typically remunerated commensurate with productivity: the more persons transported, the more a driver is paid. This is true for both drivers paid on commission and owner-operators and lessee-drivers. Only in the few cases in which they work for an hourly wage are taxi drivers paid regardless of the number of passenger-miles that they provide. In contrast, transit labor commonly receives hourly wages plus extra pay for reporting time, overtime, and time between shifts for those drivers who have split shifts. Many transit operations also have a minimum number of hours for which a driver is paid per day. While some transit systems, such as Seattle Metro, have bargained for the right to hire part-time drivers, this practice has always been prevalent in the taxi industry.

Taxi operators, therefore, enjoy two important economic advantages over transit operators with respect to labor costs. First, labor costs are hinged on productivity, and, second, labor is more flexible. Thus, even though a taxi operator might use vehicles similar to those used by a transit operator for a given paratransit service, the taxi operator should experience lower unit costs. This expectation has consistently been upheld in cases in which transit and taxi operators have bid on services. In fact, in their analysis of paratransit systems in the United States, Systan compared fifty public dial-a-bus systems with twenty-eight shared-ride taxi services. The median dial-a-bus productivity was 5.9 passengers per hour compared with 5.5 for the taxi systems. The taxi systems, however, still achieved a lower per-passenger cost, $1.70 compared with $1.82.[2]

While integrated taxi-transit services could help alleviate transit problems, they could also be the salvation of the taxi industry. For an industry experiencing financial problems, the opportunity to receive public transit funds could mean financial survival. Unfortunately for taxi operators, this opportunity is seldomly available. Until recently, federal policy has done little to foster transit-taxi cooperation. The long-promised UMTA paratransit policy statement has not been finalized after more than four years of discussion, although the Reagan administration has promised to issue it soon. Federal leadership in encouraging transit authorities to experiment with contracts with private operators has been limited to the funding of demonstration projects. For transit authorities the limited funding and the rigors of section 13c provide—in the absence of strong UMTA directives to the contrary—ample reason not to try new taxi-operated services. The resulting lack of experimentation cannot help but have adverse effects for taxi operators, transit operators, and the general public.

### SHARED-RIDE REGULATION

Taxicab regulation usually connotes restrictions on fares and the number of taxis operating in a city. These issues, which were discussed in the previous chapter, are doubtlessly important in shaping the future of the taxi industry. However, other aspects of regulation are also important.

One critical type of taxi regulation concerns shared-riding. In many, and perhaps most, cities shared-riding is legal only if the consent of the first passenger is obtained before additional passengers are picked up. As was noted in chapter 6, shared-riding was legalized as an emergency gas-saving measure during World War II. Recently, several cities have changed their ordinances to provide for shared-riding as an optional service. In some cases shared-riding is allowed at special times of the day or if advanced reservations are made. Few cities, however, have adopted regulations encouraging the adoption of shared-riding as a conventional service option.

While shared-ride service provides benefits in productivity, it provides two equally important institutional advantages. First, shared-ride service is a necessary condition for recognition by the federal government as a mass transit provider. Second, the federal fuel tax rebate is available only for taxi operators who provide shared-ride service. Thus, the provision of shared-riding is a critical criterion for taxi operators who want to become eligible for benefits. Conversely, local governments can deny those benefits by refusing to legalize shared-riding. The failure of governments to act on this problem has done a serious disservice to the taxicab industry and limited the transportation services that could be made available to the public.

### INDEPENDENT CONTRACTOR STATUS

As will be discussed later in this chapter, taxi operators have increasingly chosen to employ lessee-driver and owner-driver arrangements to organize their firms. Many of the advantages of such arrangements depend, however, on the drivers being considered by federal and state agencies to be "independent contractors" rather than "employees."

The determination of whether a driver is an independent contractor or an employee is not a simple matter. The question has been dealt with by the courts on many occasions. According to a statement by a United States circuit court of appeals: "The employer-employee relationship exists only where the person, for whom the work is done, has the right to control and direct the work, not only as to the result to be accomplished by the work, but also as to the details and means by which that result is accomplished. . . . It is the right and not the exercise of control which is the determining element."[3] This 1942 statement was not directed toward the taxi industry, but it lays out the legal principle governing whether a worker is an employee, namely whether a supervisor has the right to control how the worker conducts the work. It is significant that the court distinguished between control over the results of the work and how the work is accomplished. Only in the latter instance does control mean that the worker is an employee.

For the taxi industry, there are several controls over drivers. Fleets have work rules governing driver conduct and working hours. Cities have taxi ordinances requiring drivers to adhere to certain requirements, such as completing drive-trip sheets. States also have requirements governing working conditions and worker benefits. These various requirements mean that the question of whether a worker is "controlled" is not easily answered.

Further, the decision of whether a worker is an independent contractor is not made by only one body. The National Labor Relations Board (NLRB) makes such decisions in the context of the National Labor Relations Act governing workers' rights for collective bargaining. The Internal Revenue Service (IRS) also makes rulings about whether taxes should be withheld from a worker's pay. In addition, various state and federal agencies rule on Workmen's Compensation coverage, overtime payments, and working conditions. Thus, one or more agencies may rule that a worker is an employee, while other agencies consider the worker to be an independent contractor. In addition, a taxi operator may attempt to comply with local taxi ordinances and in so doing may be considered by the NLRB or IRS to be an employer even though he is leasing cabs to his drivers. The existence of such ambiguities means that the courts have had to rule on some of these issues.

In several cases involving taxi firms the courts have generally upheld the principle that the "right of control" over the worker is the criterion for making a worker an employee.[4] Only one case has thus far gone to the United States Court of Appeals. This case is one in which Yellow Cab Company and Checker Taxi Company, Inc., in Chicago appealed a NLRB ruling that lease drivers for these firms were employees.[5] In this case the court affirmed the "right of control" principle and rejected the contention that compliance with local taxi ordinances constituted control over how the driver conducted his or her work. It discussed the requirement that a driver keep a trip sheet and determined that such a requirement constituted control only when required by the operator but not by local laws. Further, the court ruled that a restriction by the firms that drivers not exceed 250 miles per day did not constitute control over the drivers.

This decision provides legal guidance for other similar cases, but it by no means ends the legal controversy over independent contractor status in the taxi industry. While the Yellow Cab–Checker Taxi case was decided in favor of the taxi companies, the NLRB has made rulings in other cases that lessee-drivers are employees. In one recent case the NLRB used the mere existence of a dispatching service as one of five reasons for ruling that lessee-drivers were employees. A second reason in the same case was that the firm's bookkeeping office was open for the drivers only 22.5 hours per day, meaning that for the other 1.5 hours the drivers were prohibited from transacting their business and, hence, were "controlled." Other agencies also continue to make such rulings. It is likely, therefore, that taxi operators will continue to be involved in court cases over the legal status of independent contractor drivers.

One conclusion that one might draw from all this is that the lease agreement between an operator and a driver must be carefully written to avoid requirements that may be inferred to constitute control over the driver. Requiring uniforms or a dress code are clear examples of control. Requiring data on trips and revenues is another example, as is requiring drivers to accept dispatched trips.

While the firm can do much to determine whether a driver is an independent contractor, it does not have complete authority. The public sector, through taxi ordinances and contracts with taxi operators, also influences the classification of drivers. The most common hindrance is the requirement in some taxi ordinances for a taxi firm to maintain data and records on a driver's trips. While it is desirable to keep driver manifests to aid police investigations, the question is who should keep such records. An ordinance requiring the firm to keep them can be used as evidence of the operator's control over the driver. However, no such interpretation is possible if the ordinance requires the driver to keep such data.

The issue of operating data becomes a problem in some contracts between public agencies and taxi operators. Public agencies usually need and demand operating data to be kept so as to monitor and evaluate publicly funded transportation services. However, for a taxi operator to agree to collect such operating data may constitute evidence of control over his or her drivers. An example is an airport contract in which a taxi operator agrees to pay the airport on the basis of numbers of persons picked up there or in which the taxi operator agrees to supply taxis during given hours each day. These contracts, which have long been common, cause no difficulty if the drivers are paid on a commission basis or an hourly basis, but if they are to be independent contractors, such contracts may present problems.

The issue of independent contractors is no doubt of far greater importance to the taxi industry than it is to public sector agencies. The IRS, for example, has a practical reason for wanting to limit independent contractors: employers withhold—and thereby collect—taxes for employees, but independent contractors may underreport taxable earnings. For the taxi industry, however, policies for the determination of independent contractor status are critical. Government rulings regarding independent contractor status are extremely important in determining whether leasing will become the predominant organizational form within the taxi industry.

## MANAGEMENT ACTIONS AFFECTING THE FUTURE OF THE INDUSTRY

The future of the taxi industry is not dependent only upon governmental decisions; the management skills and decisions of taxi operators will largely determine how and if the taxi industry grows and changes. The following pages discuss a few of the primary issues which taxi management must resolve.

### ORGANIZATIONAL STRUCTURE

Successful taxi firms of the future may be organized differently from those of the past. In general, success in the future is likely to depend upon greater public relations and marketing activities, as well as upon changes in driver status and personnel policies.

As discussed above, taxi operators have increasingly switched to leasing and to owner-drivers. In addition, driver-owned cooperatives have been organized in San Diego, Denver, San Francisco, Philadelphia, and elsewhere. Associations of owner-operators exist in many cities. While from a historical perspective none of these organizational forms is new, the growing number of such arrangements indicates that the industry is undergoing a transition.

For the taxi operator, there is an obvious reason for switching to lessee-driver or owner-driver arrangements. If the drivers are not ruled to be employees, the operator does not have to withhold taxes or pay Social Security, Workmen's Compensation, and other benefits. Labor and bookkeeping costs are also reduced. Operators also maintain that lessee-drivers and owner-drivers take better care of their vehicles and work harder.

From the driver's standpoint, there are also advantages to independent contractor status. One advantage is greater autonomy, long an important quality in a profession which prides itself on independence. Lessee-drivers and owner-drivers frequently market their services with local businesses and set up standing orders that never go through the firm's dispatching service. Such drivers ask for dispatched trips only when they are otherwise idle. The drivers often sublease their vehicles to other drivers for a second shift each day or on weekends. Collectively, but independent of the firm, lessee-drivers and owner-drivers often purchase the benefits that the firm usually provides for its employees. For example, they may form a drivers' association or union which purchases hospitalization and insurance for the drivers.

While independent contractor status confers obvious benefits on both operators and drivers, it is unclear what this arrangement means for the future organization of the industry. It is likely that the transition from employee-drivers to independent contractors will continue, at least in the short run. If so, fleets will continue to change into organizations composed of employee-drivers, owner-drivers, and lessee-drivers, and the distinctions between associations, cooperatives, and conventional firms will blur. The real issue, however, is whether fleets—regardless of their organizational form—will be replaced by owner-operators who are truly independent, that is, unaffiliated with associations, cooperatives, or firms.

The answer to this question depends largely on the existence of economies of scale within the industry. If there are no economic advantages to larger, more centralized firms, then the growth of unaffiliated independent contractors is likely to continue. In this case, the industry of the future is likely to be composed of many smaller firms and unaffiliated independent operators. If, on the other hand, the economic climate favors larger firms, then the industry is likely to continue to be made up of fleets, regardless of their organizational form.

Economies of scale exist in the technology and other factors, such as government involvement, that favor larger organizations. The need to attend public meetings, respond to requests for proposals, and meet public agency requirements for information argues in favor of a larger taxi firm which can afford public relations and planning personnel and computers to handle multiple billings. Such contracts also require a diverse vehicle fleet, which again favors a larger firm. This reasoning does not imply that leasing will necessarily diminish. Rather, it suggests that the successful taxi organization will be not a loose collection of independent contractors but a tightly managed firm composed of employee-drivers, lessee-drivers, and owner-drivers. Independent owner-drivers and loose associations of owner-drivers will increasingly be at a disadvantage in competing for government contracts and will primarily serve airports and hotels.

The existence of economies of scale offers an opportunity for another kind of organizational change for taxi firms in smaller cities and towns. These firms are by necessity smaller in size than most firms in large cities. They have the same needs for marketing and planning services and computerization, but they most lack the resources needed to purchase these services. Multiple-city firms, in which local entrepreneurs purchase a franchise from the company, could offer holders of franchises the same planning, marketing, and bookkeeping services that the large firms have. This concept has yet to be tested in the taxi industry.

### DIVERSIFICATION

To understand the need for diversification in the taxi industry, one has only to consider how many service industries offer only one level and type of service at one price. Most successful service industries

## Dimensions of Change / 167

offer various levels of service at various prices, including special prices at times of high or low demand. The taxi industry, however, has traditionally offered exclusive-ride service at one price, regardless of demand levels.

To be fair, some diversification has already occurred within the industry. Table 9.1 indicates that many taxi operators have diversified into package delivery, student transportation, and other specialized contract services. This is but a first step, however. With but few exceptions, taxi firms offer the ordinary taxi passenger only one type of service at one price. As discussed in chapter 9, many types of service might be offered, particularly shared-ride services with various advance reservation requirements and fares. Such a plan would offer the consumer a choice of services rather than a single take-it-or-leave-it service level.

In some instances such service diversification is contrary to local regulation, for example, ordinances specifically forbidding shared-ride service and those setting one fare for taxi service. Many ordinances should be modified to make them more permissive of alternative service levels by legalizing shared-ride service and making established fares the *maximum* allowable fares rather than the *only* fares. Some ordinances are already sufficiently vague to allow diversification.

Diversification is a necessary step for the economic survival of the taxi industry. It produces a firm with a mixture of vehicle types and the capability of providing various types of services. Such firms will be better able to compete for public contracts, as well as to maintain a growing share of the urban transportation market.

### THE TAXICAB IMAGE

Most taxicab operators will agree that one of the major problems of the industry is the poor public image of taxicabs and taxicab drivers. Dating from the days of taxicab wars and prohibition, that image is too often one of crime and deceit. Taxi drivers operate in a difficult environment, yet receive little recognition for the dangers they face or for their role in reporting emergencies. Instead, the job of a taxi driver is too often viewed by the public as a temporary one of last resort.

This image has complicated the efforts of taxi operators to compete for public transportation contracts. Sharing this negative perception of the industry, some public officials either do not consider taxi firms as prospective bidders for service contracts or disregard their qualifications. Some urban travelers do not consider the use of taxis, because they view them as a travel means for the poor or, ironically, as a high-priced service that only the rich can afford. For many persons, their only contact with the industry is when taking a taxi to a big-city airport or when calling a taxi once during a snowstorm when their own cars were immobilized. Neither experience can be viewed as typical of the service rendered by the industry.

While most operators view the industry's public image as a problem, they do not agree on the means to improve that image. To some operators a change in the public image means costly advertising, something that few taxi operators can afford. What little advertising that does occur is done by individual operators at the local level; no national industry-wide advertising campaign exists.

Improving the public image of taxicabs need not necessitate large advertising budgets, however. One inexpensive way to change the public image is to change the names of taxi firms by replacing the word *taxicab* with *transportation* or *paratransit*. A few operators have already made this name change and report positive results. Agencies and commercial clients became more interested in discussing potential contracts with a "transportation" company than they had with a "taxicab" company. As a marketing tool, this name change is effective in making potential customers aware that the firm does more than provide exclusive-ride taxi service.

Another low-cost action to improve the public image focuses on driver quality. The driver is an important public relations agent, yet the public receives very little accurate information about taxi drivers. Few people, for example, know that many drivers are independent contractors. Likewise, few people know about how few accidents per thousand miles most drivers have or what type of training a driver receives. Drivers in many cities report accidents, crimes, and emergencies to the police, but this public service goes largely unrecognized.

One solution to this problem is to publicize exemplary drivers by giving them awards and recognition. A few firms do this by selecting a "driver-of-the-month," but such individuals rarely receive notice beyond the firm's newsletter. Making such drivers the subjects of local news releases and newspaper profiles would give them wider recognition. This publicity could focus on how long the person had driven a taxi and other facts that would inform the public that the driver is a safe, courteous professional. A plaque or emblem mounted both inside and outside of the cab would inform the public that the driver had received the driver-of-the month award for that month.

The taxi firm itself could also be the subject of public relations efforts. Few people have ever visited a taxicab firm's office or garage. Fewer, still, know about how the firm operates or the range of services that it provides. Much could be done to correct these deficiencies. Firms could hold open houses for local officials and customers at the firm's facilities, display new equipment at shopping malls, produce a series of articles on the history of the firm for the local newspapers, and print and distribute fact sheets on the firm's services and size to local officials. One taxi operator conducted a contest in which prizes were given to the best suggestions for a new taxi service; in order to complete the requirements, entrants had to read a brochure describing the services that the firm was already providing.

While these marketing actions are inexpensive, they are not free. Moreover, for taxi operators who have long focused on reducing costs, maintaining vehicles, and providing dependable service, public relations and marketing require new skills. Thus, for most taxi operators these marketing actions would mean that marketing and public relations specialists would have to be hired. Since few operators could afford a full-time specialist, operators might employ consultants or part-time specialists or join together to hire one person to market for several firms.

The issues discussed in this chapter demonstrate that the future of the taxicab industry depends not only on decisions made by taxi management but also on public policies regarding transportation. Thus the future of the industry is highly speculative. However, it is possible to outline what changes need to occur in order for the industry—and urban public transportation in general—to be revitalized. This subject is treated in the next chapter.

# 12

# THE SURVIVAL OF PRIVATE ENTERPRISE IN PUBLIC TRANSPORTATION

The taxicab industry in the United States has been undergoing a subtle yet fundamental transition. All industries must continually adapt to new conditions if they are to compete and survive economically. This process of adaptation is not, however, always a smooth one; there are periods of dramatic change and periods of relative stability. The taxicab industry has been passing through such a period of dramatic change.

The reasons for this period of change have been discussed in previous chapters. While the immediate cause is declining profits, the fundamental causes are both more numerous and less simplistic. Higher energy and other operating costs have forced operators to pass these costs on to taxi passengers through higher fares, but taxi passengers are often unable to bear higher costs and must reduce taxi usage. At the same time taxi operators have faced stiff competition from a large number of government-funded transportation programs. Taxi operators have therefore been caught in a vise of higher costs and subsidized competition.

The changes that these forces have caused are already apparent within the industry. Operators have switched to leasing and owner-driver programs to reduce payroll costs. Some have also switched to smaller vehicles so as to save fuel. Many operators have pushed for inclusion in publicly funded transit and human service transportation, and virtually all have concentrated on cutting costs by finding less expensive sources for parts and reducing nonpaid mileage.

At the industry-wide level an ironic change has taken place. An industry which has historically been rather circumspect and isolated from public decision makers, the taxi industry in the past five to ten years has become increasingly involved with state and federal governments. Indeed, the International Taxicab Association has devoted an increasing amount of its attention and resources to interactions with government agencies and Congress. In recent years the association and many taxi operators have become intimately involved in lobbying efforts in Congress and in issues such as UMTA's paratransit policy and the Department of Energy's fuel priorities. Once an industry which shunned such public sector activities and focused on such operational concerns as better radios and engines, the taxi industry has been forced to focus its efforts primarily on public sector activities.

While it is clear that change has been happening, it is less certain where these changes are taking the industry or whether they will continue at such a rapid pace. Nor is it sufficient to consider the future of only the taxi industry; what happens to taxi firms is inextricably intertwined with the future of local public transportation in general. What happens to the taxi industry will both depend on and in turn influence the future of mass transit, human service transportation, and even private automobile usage.

## VISIONS OF THE FUTURE

The typical taxicab firm of the future is likely to be very different from the fleets that have characterized the industry for so long. The industry is already changing into one in which drivers are more frequently the owners of the vehicles they drive. In some cases the drivers also own the permits or licenses for their vehicles. Regardless, the future of the industry seems to be increasing autonomy for the driver with the taxi "firm" becoming an entity which provides dispatching, maintenance, and marketing services to the driver-owners.

Despite the organizational changes within the industry, the question remains how important the taxi industry of the future will be as a service provider. One often repeated scenario for the future of taxicab services is not a hopeful one, for it parallels what happened to the private urban bus companies. According to this scenario, the taxi industry will continue to shrink. Fleet firms will be the first to disappear, and taxi service will disappear entirely in many smaller communities. The remaining taxis will primarily be owner operated and will depend primarily on airport and hotel business. Far different from John Hertz's concept of taxi service as available to ordinary persons, the industry will be almost entirely a limited-purpose limousine service. Former taxi patrons, such as the elderly and the autoless, will be served by publicly owned demand-responsive services. Many smaller cities and towns will purchase automobiles and operate them so as to meet the needs of residents formerly served by private taxi firms. And like the private bus companies, what was once a privately owned industry will largely become a publicly owned one, probably as parts of public transportation authorities.

Some elements of this scenario are already occurring. Taxi fleets have been declining, as has the number of taxis in the nation. Available information also indicates that the owner-operators and lessee-operators are becoming a proportionately larger part of the industry. Transit authorities have begun implementing paratransit services using publicly owned and operated vehicles. Finally, human service agencies have severely cut into the businesses of local taxi operators. All of these factors indicate that the analogy with the private urban bus operators is not an unrealistic one.

Yet other evidence suggests that the taxi industry need not follow the path of the private bus companies. First, the private bus companies declined in an era of minimal governmental involvement. While the highway and street construction programs obviously represented public aid to the automobile, the bus operators were relatively free of federal subsidies to their competitors. Whereas the bus companies failed primarily because of changing land-use patterns and automobile ownership, the decline of taxi ridership is partly due to governmental subsidies to competing services. Second, the private bus firms were allowed to decline severely—and in some cases to disappear—before public assistance occurred. The taxi industry, as yet, has not reached such a serious stage of decline. Finally, as noted in previous chapters, there are hopeful signs of public policy changes that may be more conducive to innovative taxi operations.

These hopeful signs suggest another, more optimistic future for the taxi industry, centered around an environment in which private operators exist profitably alongside public transit authorities. The essential ingredient of this operating environment is innovation, which would be valued and rewarded. Publicly owned transit services would be restricted to heavily traveled corridors, in which fixed-route services can achieve high productivities. Virtually all other areas, and even some supplemental services along these corridors, would be served by private operators using sedans, vans, or buses. There would be neighborhood circulation services serving shopping centers, schools, and nodal points at which regional fixed-route services would be available. During peak hours private operators would supplement fixed-route services on busy routes, and feeder systems would serve low-density areas. Overlaying all these services would be shared-ride and exclusive-ride taxi services. All of these services would be changed and improved as private operators would be rewarded for new service concepts and for the quality of service provided.

These two scenarios could not be more different. In one the taxi industry all but disappears; in the other it becomes a vibrant and vital segment of a more innovative local public transit environment. Either scenario is possible. Which in fact occurs depends largely on public policy and on how public policy changes in the future.

## PUBLIC PROGRAMS AND PRIVATE OPERATORS

Private enterprise has always been lauded by public officials, with apparent sincerity and obvious enthusiasm. Politicians at all levels of government and of all political persuasions espouse the principles of private ownership and profit. These principles obviously apply to the taxicab industry. The industry is the last privately owned segment of local public transportation and is composed of locally owned, often multigenerational, family businesses. It serves needy persons in a low-cost, nonglamorous fashion. No other industry better meets the American ideals of hard work and personal commitment.

Given this background, one would expect that the taxi industry would be the subject of favorable public policies that would encourage the survival of taxi services in the private sector. The opposite, however, appears true. The industry has had to fight for recognition in fuel priority regulations and is still struggling for fuel tax rebates. It still has not received clear policy guidance from the Department of Transportation with respect to its eligibility and priority for transit funds. Already in a straitened financial condition, the industry has had to devote substantial resources just to be recognized by government at all levels as an important and legitimate public transit mode. Far from receiving favorable public policy status, it seems to be the object of public policy neglect.

From the viewpoint of the taxi operators, this discrepancy between ideals and public policy is more than a paradox; it is a cause of frustration and confusion. With few exceptions taxi operators work extremely long hours, including weekends. They survive because of their ability to cut costs and operate efficiently. Yet they must continually compete with public programs that seem wasteful when compared with taxi services. They also are accustomed to making quick decisions without written plans and studies, yet see public agencies hold endless meetings and conduct costly studies. They have too often become convinced that public officials do not understand or are not sympathetic to private enterprise and profits. For their part, some public officials have come to view taxi operators as uncooperative and bitter. What is missing is obvious: cooperation and communication based on the realization that they share common problems and objectives.

Why does an industry of small, locally owned businesses receive such unfavorable public policy treatment? How, in fact, can politicians praise the virtues of hard work and private enterprise, yet not respond to the problems of the taxi industry? The answers to these questions lie not in philosophies but in the programs and regulations through which public philosophies are manifested. Nor does the blame rest entirely on the various governmental agencies that have contact with the industry; some of the blame also falls upon the taxi industry.

The negative image of the taxi driver as an untrustworthy person still lingers in the public mind. The truth, of course, belies this image, but taxi operators have not been successful in reeducating the general public. This failure is partly understandable; changing a negative public image is a large marketing challenge, especially for persons who excel as operators. Still, this public image must change if public officials are to understand and respond to the genuine problems that public policy imposes on taxi operators.

Part of the blame, however, rests with the public sector. One could argue that an implicit assumption of the federal transit program has been public ownership of transit systems. Indeed, federal transit funds are given only to public agencies, and even though public agencies may in turn contract with private operators, they have little legislative or administrative incentive to do so. Instead, section 13c and the difficulties of bidding and contracting have provided an incentive for *not* including private operators as providers of services. The point here is a simple one: Without a strong public policy to use private operators wherever possible, public ownership will remain a more attractive, practical choice for local recipients of transit funds.

Regardless of the causes, a discrepancy has arisen between public ideals of private enterprise, hard work, and commitment, on the one hand, and the mechanics of federal transit programs, on the other. This discrepancy has hindered taxi operators in their struggle to survive, much less expand and diversify. It has also inhibited transit agencies in experimenting with innovative services and prevented their being able to cut deficits. Most of all, it has marked transit in the eyes of the consumer as something less than innovative and vibrant. The future of the taxi industry, and of transit in general, depends in a large measure on the extent to which this problem can be corrected.

## A WAY TO THE FUTURE

A dominant theme of this book has been that the taxicab industry can again become a financially healthy industry and that this revitalization is essential to the solution of some of the problems facing local public transportation. Before this revitalization can occur, however, a number of important changes must take place—some by taxi operators and some by governmental agencies.

Simply put, taxi firms must become more diversified and more market oriented. The infusion of governmental funds into local transportation necessitates both changes. To be successful, operators must

176 / The Taxicab

*An experimental paratransit vehicle of the late 1970s. This Oldsmobile Omega was modified to lengthen it and raise the roof. (International Taxicab Association.)*

*Interior of an experimental paratransit vehicle showing access for wheelchair passengers. (International Taxicab Association.)*

*An experimental paratransit vehicle of the late 1970s, this one built by Alfa-Romeo. (International Taxicab Association.)*

increasingly diversify to serve special school children, the elderly, the handicapped, and other groups targeted by governmental programs. Taxi operators must also aggressively push shared-riding as a service alternative for exclusive-ride patrons. In short, the industry must offer more types of service. This diversification also means new types of vehicles are necessary. Unfortunately, Checker Motors Corporation announced in April 1982 that it was considering discontinuing the manufacturing of taxicabs. As the only taxicab capable of holding five passengers in the rear, the Checker is an important vehicle for shared-ride service, and its demise might hinder the development of shared-riding. Energy costs alone have necessitated smaller vehicles for exclusive-ride services. Offering a wider range of services means that small cars, full-size sedans, vans, and small buses will become necessary elements in a taxi fleet. Indeed, progressive operators are already diversifying their fleets.

These changes will make little difference, however, if they are not accompanied by aggressive marketing efforts. Diversification implies a change from a "taxicab operation" to a full-service "transportation provider." Yet if out-dated, negative public images persist, the benefits of diversification will not be realized. It is not sufficient merely to diversify; operators must also inform and educate the public.

The challenge of marketing is a new one for most taxi operators, who have been trained to concentrate on providing efficient service at minimum cost. In fact, marketing can be costly, a fact which is in conflict with the cost-conscious orientation of many operators. It need not, however, be very costly; low-cost but effective marketing strategies are available.

The change to diversified, market-oriented firms means significant changes in taxi operations. In particular, taxi operators will experience higher costs in the time they spend in dealing with a variety of public agencies. Operators who have already contracted with public agencies have quickly recognized this. Payments from agencies are notoriously late, meaning a real financial cost to operators. Interaction with the public sector necessitates more letters, reports, plans, and operating data, all of which usually exceed the operator's own needs. These, too, are costly. Finally, meetings are almost always more numerous and less productive than operators anticipate.

While necessary, these changes in taxi operations alone will not ensure the revival of the taxi industry; public sector changes are also required. These changes are numerous, but they all are directed toward the same objective: creating an operating environment in which taxicab operators can fairly compete and in which they are rewarded for efficiency, initiative, and hard work.

The recent changes in federal transit policies may or may not be a first step toward this objective. Current federal transit policy calls for a termination of federal operating assistance in fiscal year 1983 for cities under fifty thousand population and two years later for larger cities. Federal capital assistance will be continued and even increased. Federal regulations will also be reduced or eased, including sections 13c and 504. The intent of these changes is to decrease the role of the federal government in the provision of transit services.

For taxicab operators these changes represent a hopeful sign. Transit programs will be controlled more at the local level, a level at which taxi operators have had long experience in dealing with government. In addition, the importance of section 13c as a hindrance to service integration may be reduced. Thus, transit systems faced with a cutoff of federal operating assistance may enter into more joint ventures with taxi operators as a means of retaining services.

These changes in federal policy suggest another less optimistic possibility. Many states and cities may refuse to increase their transit operating assistance to compensate for the federal cutoff. Rather than contract with private taxi operators, transit systems faced with reduced funding may simply cut service. The result may be more trips by automobile, with taxicab operators in worse condition than now.

Whether the federal policy changes lead to a more vibrant taxicab industry depends at least in part on how local governments and taxicab operators are able to achieve better communication. One important but usually overlooked public sector role is fostering communication between local transportation providers, planners, regulators, and decision makers. Such communication occurs frequently between transit operators and planners, but at the local level distrust, rather than communication, is too often the rule with respect to taxi operators and the other groups. Local and state transportation associations, yearly state-wide conferences, monthly meetings, and informal discussions—all can play a role in dispelling mistrust and focusing discussion on common transportation service problems.

A second public sector change is a philosophical one. The concept of profit, and, hence, of private ownership, long ago vanished from the mass transit industry. Consequently, many public officials believe in private enterprise but have long since stopped thinking about it in the context of local public transportation. This thinking must change. Profits must be encouraged so as to attract high-quality management personnel into the taxi industry, and private ownership must be given serious consideration as a viable alternative to public ownership.

Most important, however, changes must be made in public policies that affect the industry. Fuel tax rebates should be the rule rather than the exception. Local regulations should be updated and made more positive so as to encourage rather than suppress initiative by taxi operators. States should make coordination of human service transportation a requirement and stipulate that taxi operators be given a chance to bid on coordinated services. And, of course, the federal government should clearly and forcefully require the same opportunity for taxi operators wishing to participate in transit programs.

These changes, by both taxi operators and the public sector, are easy to list. They are not so easy to implement, for they require hard work and considerable human energy. Most of all, however, they require a commitment by everyone concerned to the goal of local public transportation services that are more effective, less costly, and considerably more creative.

# NOTES

## CHAPTER 2

1. *Chamber's Encyclopaedia*, 1738, "The Thames wherry is stoutly built and is constructed to carry eight passengers. It is usually managed by one sculler or two oarsmen." Pepys's *Diary* also includes a reference to wherries in 1666.
2. Mumford, *City in History*, p. 62.
3. Gutkind, *International History*, 5:244, 6:456.
4. Pushkarev and Zupan, *Public Transportation*, p. 6.
5. Leighton, *Transportation and Communication*, pp. 108–9.
6. Gutkind, *International History*, 6:457, 465.
7. Ibid., 5:244.
8. Moore, *Omnibuses*, p. 182.
9. *The Romaunt of the Rose*, 1137, "He . . . loved to have welle hors of prys. He wende to have reproved be Of thefte or moordrye, if that he Hadde in his stable only hakeney" (chap. 4, p. 2).
10. Moore, *Omnibuses*, p. 196.
11. It can be seen from this letter (written six years before the enactment of the London Hackney Carriage Act, 1831, *1 and 2 William 4, c. 22*) that there must have been a regulation requiring the printing of a list of fares. This letter is quoted by Moore, *Omnibuses*, p. 200.
12. Chief Justice Whaite speaking for the court in *Munn vs. Illinois*, 94 U.S. 113.
13. Proclamation by Charles I, 19 January 1635.
14. Pepys, *Diary*, 7 November 1660.
15. Stratton, *World on Wheels*, p. 15.
16. Dunbar, *Buses, Trolleys, Trams*, p. 10.
17. Ibid., p. 19.
18. Ibid.
19. Stratton, *World on Wheels*, p. 15.
20. Taylor, "The Beginnings," pt. 1, p. 45.
21. Dunbar, *Buses, Trolleys, Trams*, p. 17.
22. The word received official recognition in the title of the London Cab Act of 1896.
23. Moore, *Omnibuses*, p. 212.
24. The term *hackney cab* referred to vehicles built to carry for-hire passengers, while *hackney coach* referred to the hackney vehicles that had previously been used as family coaches.

25. Dickens, *Sketches by Boz*, scene 7.
26. Moore, *Omnibuses*, p. 218.
27. The Hebrew word pronounced "shāphēl" means "low." The German word *shofel* means "base," "mean," or "worthless."
28. Mayhew in *London Labour II* said "I don't think these 'shofuls' [hansoms] should be allowed." In *III* he said: "Hansom's . . . are always called showfulls by the cabmen. 'Showfull,' in slang, means counterfeit, and the 'showfull' cabs are an infringement on Hansom's patent." In 1862, at an international exhibit, the vehicle was described as "the shofle or gentleman's Hansom" and another vehicle as "the new Brougham 'shofle.'"
29. It may be that the name was bestowed on the carriage by the French.
30. The "calash" ("calèche" in French) was a seventeenth-century carriage with a folding top.

## CHAPTER 3

1. U.S. Bureau of the Census, *Historical Statistics*, pp. 8–44.
2. Glaab and Brown, *History*, p. 139.
3. Ibid., p. 135.
4. Clark, *Population Growth*, p. 340.
5. Ibid.
6. Weber, *Growth of Cities*, p. 468.
7. Clark, *Population Growth*, p. 340.
8. Glaab and Brown, *History*, p. 159.
9. The variations in density estimates from study to study no doubt reflect different definitions of density, as well as uncertain data.
10. Glaab and Brown, *History*, p. 159.
11. Ibid., p. 148.
12. Taylor, "Beginnings," pt. 2, p. 34.
13. Smerk, *Development*, pp. 6–7.
14. Taylor, "Beginnings," pt. 2, p. 39.
15. Glaab and Brown, *History*, p. 149.
16. Ibid., p. 150.
17. Rae, *American Automobile*, pp. 2–3.
18. Smerk, *Development*, pp. 6–7.
19. Glaab and Brown, *History*, p. 150.
20. Ibid.
21. Ibid., p. 151.
22. Ibid., p. 152.
23. Warner, *Streetcar Suburbs*.
24. Glaab and Brown, *History*, p. 154.
25. Weber, *Growth of Cities*, p. 469.
26. Ibid.
27. Rae, *American Automobile*, is an excellent description of the development of the

automobile and is the source for much of the material in this section.
28. Rae, *American Automobile*, p. 1.
29. Ibid., p. 61.
30. Vidich, *New York Cab Driver*.
31. Moore, *Omnibuses*.
32. Vidich, *New York Cab Driver*, p. 58.
33. Freeman, "Horseless Fiacre," p. 28.

## CHAPTER 4

1. Goodman and Freund, *Principles*, p. 24.
2. Interview with Walter Jacobs, 26 June 1981.
3. *Business Week*, "Once Lowly Taxi," pp. 22–24.
4. An interesting aside is that the Checker-GM battle in New York City almost was prevented. In 1930, J. J. Rascob, who had 10 percent of the syndicate that financed Checker's expansion, urged GM to purchase Checker Motors. The Fisher brothers, who were important GM directors and heads of the GM body manufacturing division, blocked the purchase. Instead, GM chose to make their disastrous entry into the New York City taxicab industry to protect their share of the market there.
5. Interview with Ralph E. Oakland, 29 November 1979.
6. Ibid.
7. *Essential Link*, p. 14.
8. Interview with Frank Sawyer, 13 December 1979.
9. Much of the history of the Rothschild's taxi business is based on an interview with John Petit, 10 December 1979.
10. Interview with Frank Sawyer, 13 December 1979.

## CHAPTER 5

1. Saltzman, "Decline of Transit," pp. 24–29.
2. Solomon and Saltzman, "History of Transit."
3. Wilcox, *Analysis of the Electric Railway Problem*, p. 102.
4. Ibid.
5. Saltzman, "Decline of Transit," pp. 24–29.
6. Simpson, "Taxicab Problem," pp. 14–15.
7. Vidich, *New York Cab Driver*, pp. 68–69.
8. Tompkins, "Taxicab Runs Amuck," p. 387.
9. Vidich, *New York Cab Driver*, p. 71.
10. *Business Week*, 28 December 1932, p. 9.
11. In one city, Baltimore, Tompkins (1932) reported that the taxicab accident rate grew by 140 percent between 1931 and 1932.
12. Simpson, "Taxicab Problem," p. 1.

13. Ibid., p. 21.
14. Records at International Taxicab Association.
15. Nearly 2,000 of these were soon turned back to the city, leaving the total at 11,787.
16. Simpson, "Taxicab Problem," p. 13.

## CHAPTER 6

1. American Public Transit Association, *Factbook*.
2. Simpson, "War's Impact," pp. 467–68.
3. *American City*, March 1941, pp. 95–96.
4. Ibid.
5. Cab Research Bureau, "Taxicab Adequacy."
6. International City Managers Association, *Municipal Yearbook*, p. 421.
7. *Business Week*, 17 February 1945, p. 36.
8. *Business Week*, 25 December 1943, p. 48.
9. *Business Week*, 5 September 1942, p. 36.
10. *Business Week*, 27 February 1943, p. 24.
11. *Business Week*, 3 August 1946, pp. 31–33.
12. *New York Times*, 18 January 1946, p. 6.
13. *Taxi Weekly*, 6 March 1947, p. 7.
14. International City Managers Association, *Municipal Yearbook*, pp. 416–24.
15. Cab Research Bureau, "Taxicab Adequacy."

## CHAPTER 7

1. Simpson, "War's Impact," pp. 467–68.
2. U.S. Bureau of the Census, *Historical Statistics*, p. 721.
3. Smerk, *Urban Mass Transportation*, p. 142.
4. Mossman, *Principles*, p. 9.
5. American Public Transit Association, *Factbook*.
6. For a detailed account of how this act was passed, see Smerk, *Urban Mass Transportation*, chap. 1.
7. Federal operating assistance is scheduled to end after fiscal year 1982 for cities under fifty thousand and after fiscal year 1984 for larger cities.
8. Rogoff, "Regulation," p. 9.
9. Ibid.
10. American Public Transit Association, *Factbook*.

## CHAPTER 8

1. Wells, "Analysis," and "Taxicab Operating." Most operators keep careful records of key financial and operating data. Unfortunately, these data are not generally available either to other operators or to persons outside the industry who need to understand the conditions facing taxi operators. The federal government collects no taxi operating data, and only a few states attempt to do so. In fact, most taxi operators report operating data only when necessary to support taxi fare increase requests. As a result, no systematic, on-going taxi data reporting system exists. Consequently, in attempting to understand the economic conditions within the industry, one must rely on fragmentary data collected by a few local and state governments or on two national surveys of taxi operators. These two surveys cover the years 1973 and 1975 and are no longer timely; they are used extensively in this chapter, however, because they are the best available sources of national data. Another national survey is being conducted as this book goes to print, but the results of this survey are not yet available.
2. For the 1973 survey, 10.8 percent (675 firms) responded; for 1975, 4.7 percent (245 firms) responded.
3. Ellis, "Taxicab Industry," p. 21, appendix 2.
4. Inventories conducted by each of these states resulted in these estimates.
5. Ellis, "Taxicab Industry," p. 21, appendix 2.
6. Busath, *Characteristics*, appendix G.
7. Northeastern Illinois Planning Commission, "Taxicabs and Dial-a-Bus," p. 22.
8. Wells, "Taxicab Operating."
9. Gilbert et al., "Taxicab User."
10. Busath, *Characteristics*, p. 10.
11. Northeastern Illinois Planning Commission, "Taxicabs and Dial-a-Bus," p. 32. The NIPC used home interview data and could not estimate street miles.
12. Wells, "Taxicab Operating." The cost per mile for firms with 100 to 199 cabs was only $.27, but this category was dominated by lease operations.
13. Ibid.
14. Busath, *Characteristics*, pp. 11–12.
15. Wells, "Taxicab Operating."
16. Busath, *Characteristics*, pp. 11–12.
17. Northeastern Illinois Planning Commission, "Taxicabs and Dial-a-Bus," p. 11.
18. Wells, "Taxicab Operating."
19. International Taxicab Association, unpublished.
20. Computed by authors.
21. Wells, "Taxicab Operating."
22. Gilbert et al., "Taxicab User," p. 33.
23. Wells, "Taxicab Operating."
24. Busath, *Characteristics*, appendix K.
25. Wells, "Taxicab Operating."
26. Gilbert et al., "Taxicab User," p. 33.
27. Wells, "Taxicab Operating."

28. Ibid.
29. Ernst and Whinney, *Paratransit Energy*, p. 2:8.
30. Midendorf, Heathington, and David, "Analysis."
31. Webster, Weiner, and Wells, "Role of Taxicabs," p. vi.
32. Northeastern Illinois Planning Commission, "Taxicabs and Dial-a-Bus," p. 14.
33. Wells, "Taxicab Operating."
34. Ibid.

## CHAPTER 9

1. Systan, *Paratransit Handbook*, pp. 1–20.
2. Ibid.
3. Multisystems, *Paratransit Assessment*, 1:2–4.
4. Wells, "Analysis."
5. For a description of this program, see Multisystems, *Paratransit Assessment*, 3:21–29.

## CHAPTER 10

1. Bland, "Taxicab Ordinances," p. 9, appendix 1.
2. The states that control fares and entry into the industry are: Montana, Nevada, Colorado, Nebraska, Kentucky, Pennsylvania, Delaware, and Connecticut.
3. *New York Times*, 13 March 1980, section A, p. 1.
4. Kahn, *Economics of Regulation*, vol. 2.
5. Clark, *Competition*, pp. 174–75.

## CHAPTER 11

1. American Public Transit Association, "Excess Passenger Capacity Statement."
2. Systan, *Paratransit Handbook*, pp. 1–20.
3. *Williams* vs. *United States*, 126 F. 2d 132 (1942).
4. Examples of recent cases include: Greater Houston Transportation Company, 208 NLRB 1020; Barwood, Inc., 209 NLRB 19; and Columbus Green Cabs, Inc., 214 NLRB 751.
5. 603 F. 2d 862 (1979) and District of Columbia Court of Appeals, 20 June 1979.

# BIBLIOGRAPHY

## INTERVIEWS

Walter Jacobs (former owner of Yellow Drive-It-Urself Company). 26 June 1981
Ralph E. Oakland (financial adviser to Morris Markin). 29 November 1979
John Pettit (formerly of Yellow Cab of San Francisco). 10 December 1979
Frank Sawyer (owner of Checker Cab Company and other paratransit services in Boston). 13 December 1979

## SOURCES CONSULTED

American Public Transit Association. "Excess Passenger Capacity Statement." Washington, D.C.: American Public Transit Association, 1979.
──────. *Transit Factbook*. Washington, D.C.: American Public Transit Association, 1977.
"Beleaguered Cabs." *Business Week*, 5 September 1942, pp. 36ff.
Bland, T. E. "A Review of Local Taxicab Ordinances in North Carolina." In *Proceedings: Taxicab and Transit Conference, Winston-Salem, N.C.* Chapel Hill: University of North Carolina, Department of City and Regional Planning, 1978.
Brown, T. A. "Economic Analysis of the Taxicab Industry in Pennsylvania." Middletown, Pa.: Pennsylvania State University, Capital Campus, 1973.
Busath, K. *Characteristics of the California Taxicab Industry*. Sacramento: California Taxicab Owners Association, 1975.
"Cab Licenses Sought by 225 G.I.'s a Week." *New York Times*, 18 January 1946, sec. 1, p. 6.
Cab Research Bureau. *Taxicab Adequacy*. Cleveland: National Association of Taxicab Owners, 1942.
──────. *Taxicabs and Trends in Urban Passenger Transportation*. Cleveland: National Association of Taxicab Owners, 1955.
Chaucer, Geoffrey. *The Romaunt of the Rose*. Edited by Max Kaluza. London: K. Paul, Trench, Trubner, and Co., 1891.
Clark, Colin. *Population Growth and Land Use*. London: Macmillan, 1967.
Clark, J. M. *Competition as a Dynamic Process*. Washington, D.C.: Brookings Institution, 1961.
"Coach, Hackney Coaches." *Chambers Cyclopedia*. 2nd ed. 1738.

Dickens, Charles. *Sketches by Boz.* Cambridge, Mass.: Riverside Press, 1850.
Dunbar, Charles Stuart. *Buses, Trolleys, Trams.* 2nd ed. New York: P. Hamlyn, 1967.
Ellis, B. "The Taxicab Industry in North Carolina." In *Proceedings: Taxicab and Transit Conference, Winston-Salem, N.C.* Chapel Hill: University of North Carolina, Department of City and Regional Planning, 1978.
Ernst and Whinney. *Paratransit Energy Conservation and Contingency Study.* For North Central Texas Council of Governments. Arlington, Tex.: North Central Texas Council of Governments, 1980.
*An Essential Link in American Transportation, 1853–1953.* Chicago: Parmalee Transportation Co., 1953.
Freeman, L. "The Horseless Fiacre." *New York Times,* 26 October 1947, sec. 6, p. 28.
"G.I. Cab Ride." *Business Week,* 3 August 1946, pp. 31–33.
Gilbert, G., Fravel, F., and Di'Iorio, F. "Taxicab User Characteristics in Small and Medium-Size Cities." For U.S. Department of Transportation. Report no. UMTA-NC-11-0003. Chapel Hill: University of North Carolina, Department of City and Regional Planning, 1976.
Gilbert, G., Garber, C., and Foerster, J. E. "Establishing Innovative Taxicab Services: A Guidebook." For Urban Mass Transit Administration. Report no. UMTA-NC-11-0005. Chapel Hill: University of North Carolina, Department of City and Regional Planning, 1977.
Glaab, C. N., and Brown, A. T. *A History of Urban America.* New York: Macmillan, 1967.
Goodman, W. I., and Freund, E. C. *Principles and Practice of Urban Planning.* Washington, D.C.: International City Managers Association, 1968.
Gutkind, E. A. *International History of City Development.* 8 vols. New York: Free Press, 1970.
International City Managers Association. *Municipal Yearbook, 1948.* Washington, D.C.: International City Managers Association, 1948.
Kahn, A. E. *The Economics of Regulation: Principles and Institutions.* 2 vols. New York: Wiley, 1970.
Kendall, D. "A Comparison of Findings from Projects Employing User-Side Subsidies for Taxi and Bus Travel." For Urban Mass Transit Administration. Cambridge, Mass.: Transportation Systems Center, 1979.
Kirby, R. F., Bhatt, K. U., Kemp, M. A., and McGillivray, R. G. *Paratransit: Neglected Options for Urban Mobility.* Washington, D.C.: Urban Institute, 1974.
Leighton, A. C. *Transportation and Communication in Early Medieval Europe,* A.D. *500–1100.* New York: Barnes and Noble, 1972.
Middendorf, D. P., Heathington, K. W., and Davis, F. "An Analysis of the Demand of Bus and Shared-Ride Taxi Service in Two Smaller Urban Areas." Knoxville: University of Tennessee, Transportation Center, 1975.
Moore, Henry Charles. *Omnibuses and Cabs.* London: Chapman and Hall, 1902.
Mossman, F. H. *Principles of Urban Transportation.* Cleveland: Western Reserve University Press, 1951.
Motor Vehicle Manufacturers Association of the United States. *Facts and Figures.* Detroit: Motor Vehicle Manufacturers Association of the U.S., 1972.

Multisystems. *Paratransit Assessment and Directions for the Future*. For U.S. Department of Transportation. Washington, D.C.: Urban Mass Transit Administration, 1980.

Mumford, Lewis. *The City in History*. New York: Harcourt, Brace and World, 1961.

"New York's Taxi Industry Thriving on Some Controversial Economics." *New York Times*, 13 March 1980, sec. A, p. 1.

Northeastern Illinois Planning Commission. "Taxicabs and Dial-a-Bus: Demand Actuated Transportation in Northeastern Illinois." Chicago: Northeastern Illinois Planning Commission, 1976.

"Once Lowly Taxi Now Wooed by Great Motor Companies." *Business Week*, 29 October 1930, pp. 22–24.

"One Taxicab per 2000 Population called Economic Ratio." *American City*, March 1941, pp. 95–96.

Pepys, Samuel. *The Diary of Samuel Pepys*. 17 vols. Edited by Henry B. Wheatley. New York: Croscup and Sterling, 1892.

Pushkarev, B. S., and Zupan, J. M. *Public Transportation and Land Use Policy*. Bloomington: Indiana University Press, 1977.

Rae, J. F. *The American Automobile: A Brief History*. Chicago: University of Chicago Press, 1965.

Rogoff, E. G. "Regulation of the New York City Taxicab Industry." *City Almanac*, vol. 15, no. 2, p. 19.

Saltzman, A. "The Decline of Transit." In *Public Transportation: Planning Operations, and Management*. Edited by L. Hoel and G. Gray. Englewood Cliffs, N.J.: Prentice-Hall, 1979.

Simpson, F. R. "The War's Impact on Urban Transit Systems." *Harvard Business Review* (summer 1945): 460–68.

Simpson, H. S. "The Taxicab Problem." Bulletin no. 389. N.p.: American Electric Railway Association, 1932.

Smerk, G. M. "The Development of Public Transportation and the City." In *Public Transportation Planning, Operations, and Management*. Edited by L. Hoel and G. Gray. Englewood Cliffs, N.J.: Prentice-Hall, 1979.

―――. *Urban Mass Transportation: A Dozen Years of Federal Policy*. Bloomington: Indiana University Press, 1974.

Solomon, R. J., and Saltzman, A. "History of Transit and Innovative Systems." Report TR-70-20. Cambridge, Mass.: Urban Systems Laboratory, Massachusetts Institute of Technology, 1971.

Stratton, E. M. *The World on Wheels*. New York: published by the author, 1878.

Systan, Inc. *Paratransit Handbook*. For U.S. Department of Transportation. Washington, D.C.: Urban Mass Transit Administration, 1979.

"Taxi." *Business Week*, 28 December 1932, p. 9.

"Taxi Dilemma." *Business Week*, 27 February 1943, pp. 24ff.

"Taxis Do Well." *Business Week*, 25 December 1943, p. 48ff.

"Taxis Needed." *Business Week*, 17 February 1945, p. 36.

*Taxi Weekly*. Untitled article. 6 March 1947, p. 7.

Taylor, G. R. "The Beginnings of Mass Transit in America." *Smithsonian Journal of History* 1 (1966): part 1, p. 44; part 2, p. 34.
Tompkins, R. S. "The Taxicab Runs Amuck." *American Mercury*, 26 August 1932, pp. 385-94.
"Trafficking in Taxis." *Barron's*, 23 February 1981, p. 16.
U.S. Bureau of the Census. *Historical Statistics of the United States*. Vol. 1. Washington, D.C.: Government Printing Office, 1975.
Vidich, Charles. *The New York Cab Driver and His Fare*. Cambridge, Mass.: Schenkman, 1976.
Warner, S. B. *Streetcar Suburbs: The Process of Growth in Boston*. Cambridge: Massachusetts Institute of Technology and Harvard University, 1962.
Weber, A. F. *The Growth of Cities in the Nineteenth Century*. Reprint. Ithaca: Cornell University Press, 1963.
Webster, A., Weiner, E., and Wells, J. "The Role of Taxicabs in Urban Transportation." For U.S. Department of Transportation. Washington, D.C.: Office of Transportation Planning Analysis, 1974.
Wells, J. D. "Analysis of Taxicab Operating Characteristics." Rockville, Md.: International Taxicab Association, 1975.
───. "Taxicab Operating Statistics." For U.S. Department of Transportation. Washington, D.C.: Office of Transportation Systems Analysis, 1977.
Wilcox, D. F. *Analysis of the Electric Railway Problem*. New York: published by the author, 1921.
Wisconsin Department of Transportation. "Wisconsin Taxicabs." Madison: Wisconsin Department of Transportation, 1976.

# INDEX

Abata, Dominic, 95
Aged. *See* Elderly and handicapped persons
Airports: regulation of taxicabs at, 144–45
Allegheny County, Pa., Port Authority, 99; and social services, 137
Allen, Harry N., 34–35
Ambassador automobile, 44
American Cab Drivers Association for Discharged Veterans, 81
American Taxicab Association (ATA), 59, 83
Antitrust litigation, 82–83
Arabi, La., 134
Arcadia, Cal., 129–31
Associations of owner-drivers, 91, 165
Associations of taxicab drivers, 165
Automobiles: birth of, 31–34; electric, 31–32; steam, 31; production of, 32–33, 39, 63, 75
Avis Rent-A-Car System, Inc., 55

Back door cab, 23
Baily, Captain, 10–11
Baldi, Al, 53
Baltimore, Md., 27, 71
Barstow, Cal., 129–31
Baudry, Stanislaus, 17–18
Bell Cab Company, 58
Benz, Karl, 32
Benz taxicab, 33
Berlin, 26–27, 30, 35
Black & White cab companies, 43

Black & White Checker Taxi Company (Little Rock, Ark.), 129, 132
Boats, 8, 181 (n. 1). *See also* Wherry
Boston, Mass., 27, 30, 52–55, 70, 143, 146
Bridgeport, Conn., 63
Brokerage, 137, 159
Brown, T. A., 26, 30
Bruhn, Wilhelm, 35
Buick, David, 32
Bureau of the Census, 110
Bus (motorbus), 25, 43, 64–65; manufacture of, 43; ridership of, 65, 84
Busath, K., 116–17
Busch, Adolphus, 32

Cab, 19, 23–24, 35–36. *See also* Cabriolet; Taxicab
Cab Drivers Union (London), 35
Cable car, 29
Cabriolet, 19–20, 23, 25. *See also* Cab
Caddies, 12
California, 112–18 passim, 128, 134
Car pooling, 123
Certificate of Public Convenience and Necessity, 71
Chairs, 11, 12
Chapel Hill, N.C., 134
Chapman, John, 22
Chariots, 13
Charles I: patent for sedan chairs granted by, 11; limitation of hackney licenses by, 15
Charles II: ban on plying for hire by, 15; limitation of hackney licenses by, 15

Charon, 8
Chaucer, Geoffrey, 10
Chauffeurs. *See* Drivers
Checker cab, 50–54, 69, 75–76, 85, 177
Checker Cab Company (Los Angeles), 53
Checker Cab Manufacturing Company (Checker Motors Corporation), 48–56 passim, 76, 85, 177
Checker Taxi Company, Inc. (Chicago), 52, 66, 69, 81, 83, 95, 104
Checker Taxi Company of Boston, 52–55
Chicago, Ill., 27, 29, 40–53 passim, 56, 58, 65–66, 69, 75, 78, 95, 81–83, 112–15, 138, 143
Chicago Motor Coach Company, 43, 45, 48
Chicago Yellow Cab Company, Inc. (Walden W. Shaw Livery Company), 40, 42, 50–52, 57, 87, 95
Ch'in Dynasty, 13
Civil Aeronautics Act of 1938, 62
Clarence, 23
Claremont, Cal., 130–31
Clark, Colin, 26, 149
Cleveland, Ohio, 53
Cocher de fiacre, 11
Columbus, Ohio, 58
Commissions, 94, 103. *See also* Drivers, Commissions
Commonwealth Motors Company, 49
Compression ignition (diesel) engine, 32
Conventional taxi service. *See* Taxicab service, exclusive ride
Cooperatives, 165
Copley Tours, 55
Costs. *See* Economics of taxicab operations
Cottage industries, 9
Cream skimming, 151, 152
Cruising, 11
Cugnot, Nicholas, 31
Cugnot automobile, 31

Daimler, Gottlieb, 32
Daley, Jack, Jr., 58
Daley, Jack, Sr., 58
Dallas, Tex., 116–18
Danville, Ill., 138
Darracq automobile, 35
Davenport, Iowa, 114–15
Davis, Charles, 53
Deadheading, 42
Demand characteristics, 110–12; wartime, 76, 79; levels of, 110; of passengers, 110–12; of trips, 112–13. *See also* Economics of taxicab operations
Democratic Union Organizing Committee, Local 777, 95
Denver, Colo., 53, 114–15, 165
Department of Energy (DOE), 171
Department of Health and Human Services (HHS), 157
Department of Justice, 82, 86–87
Department of Labor (DOL), 101, 157
Department of Transportation (DOT), 36, 90; funding by, 91, 96–97, 135, 137, 139
Depression, 52, 55, 60–74 passim, 141–49 passim; chaos and regulation during, 61–73, 141–48; transportation, effect on, 61–73, 81; unemployment during, 61; insurance required during, 66
Deregulation, 141–47. *See also* Entry controls; Open entry; Regulation
Des Moines, Iowa, 31
De Soto taxicabs, 50, 76, 85
Dickens, Charles, 20–22
Dial-a-bus, 5, 123–24, 128. *See also* Paratransit; Taxicab services
Dial-a-ride, 5, 123–24, 128, 134; costs of, 119. *See also* Taxicab services
Diesel, Rudolph, 32
Diesel engine, 32
Dilger, Frank, 52
Dispatching, 42, 83, 119, 127; by telephone, 42; by radio, 83; shared

Diversification. *See* Taxicab services
Dodge, Henry, 32
Dodge, John, 32
Dodge taxicabs, 50
Drivers, 3, 10–17, 41–42, 52–54, 66–68, 73, 91, 94–96, 103–6, 119, 159, 165; of hackneys, 10, 12, 16–17, 34, 54; regulation of, 15–17, 142; and liability for damages, 17; licensing of, 17, 66–68; commissions, 41, 94, 103, 159; as owners, 52, 91, 94, 103–6, 165; unemployment of, 66; unions of, 94–96, 105; fringe benefits for, 94, 103, 165; as lessees, 103–6, 165; as employees, 103–6, 165; labor costs of, 119, 159; part-time, 159, 165; cooperatives of, 165. *See also* Independent contractor
Duke of Clarence, 23
Dunbar, 17
Duncomb, Sir Saunders, 11–12
Duryea, Charles, 32
Duryea, Frank, 32

Economics of taxicab operations, 103–22 passim, 150–66 passim; fares, 66–68, 113–17, 129; demand characteristics, 76, 79, 110–11; industry organization, 103–8; supply characteristics, 108–10; levels of demand, 110; passenger characteristics, 110–12, 125; costs, 116–19; revenues, 117–18; profitability, 119–20; performance characteristics, 120–22; trends and the future, 122; and natural monopoly, 145–51; deregulation, 145–47; economies of scale, 150, 166. *See also* Deregulation; Regulation; Taxicab operations
Egypt, 8
El Cajon, Cal., 130–31
Elderly and handicapped persons, 3, 96–97, 125–29, 135–37, 176; under section 16 of UMT Act, 96
Electric automobile, 31

Electric cabs, 31–36
Electric Carriage & Wagon Company, 33–34
Electric engine, 30
Electric Railway Presidents' Conference, 64–65
Electric starter, 31
Electric Storage Battery Company (Electric Vehicle Company), 31–34
Electrobat, 31, 33
Emergency Transportation Act of 1933, 61
Entry controls, 66–67, 70–72, 80–83, 141–50, 155. *See also* Open entry; Regulation
Exclusive ride. *See* Taxicab services, exclusive ride
Fares, 41, 60, 66–71, 113–18, 127, 129, 132–33, 141–55; of hackneys, 13, 41; of omnibuses, 18; calculation of, by taximeter, 113, 116; calculation of, by zone rates, 113, 116; flat rates, 113, 116; calculation of, by schedule of variable rates, 133. *See also* Economics of taxicab operations, fares; Mass transit, fares
Federal Communications Commission (FCC), 86
Federal competition with paratransit, 72, 94, 96, 119
Federal funding of mass transit, 87–91, 100–102, 128–38, 156–58. *See also* Urban Mass Transportation Act
Federal government. *See* United States government
Federal Highway Administration (FHWA), 91
Federal regulation, 86–87, 99, 100; and minimum wage, 152
Federal Trade Commission (FTC), 86
Federal transit policy of DOT, 96–100
Feeder service. *See* Taxicab services
Feldman, Jeffrey, 58

Feldman, Jerry E., 58
Fiacre, 11
Field, Marshall, 51
Fifth Avenue Coach Company, 43, 48
Financial responsibility. *See* Insurance
Firestone Tire & Rubber Company, 43–44
Fisher Brothers, 183 (chap. 4, n. 4)
Fixed-route transit. *See* Mass transit
Flat rates. *See* Taxicab operations
Fleets. *See* Taxicabs
Ford, Henry, 32
Ford automobile, 32, 44
Ford taxicab, 54
Foreman, Alfred, 44
Franchise: Yellow Cab name, 43; licenses, Los Angeles, Cal., 80; Chicago taxicab companies, 81
Franklin taxicab, 54
Free entry. *See* Open entry

Gallieni, Joseph Simon, 37
General Cab Company, 48, 50
General market services, 128–35. *See also* Taxicab services
General Motors Corporation, 48–50, 183 (chap. 4, n. 4)
General Omnibus Company, 18
George III, 16, 18
Gilbert, Gorman, 112, 117–18
Giligulicha, 13
Glabb, C. N., 26, 30
Glassman, Marvin, 58
Glassman, Max, 58
Glimco, Joseph, 95
Gray, Charles, 57
Green, George A., 43
Grip car, 29
Growler, 34. *See also* Hansom Cabs
Gutkind, E. A., 19

Haas Law, 71, 92
Hackney, 10–14, 19–25; lease of, 10; license required, 10, 16; livery, 10, 54; standings, 10, 11, 20; coach, 12, 181 (n. 24); cab, 13, 181 (n. 24); fares charged, 13; regulation of, 14–17; fixed routes of, 17–19; showfuls, 22, 182 (nn. 27, 28)
Hadley Knight Company, 50
Hailed ride. *See* Taxicab services
Hansom, Joseph, 22
Hansom Cab, 22–25, 34–36. *See also* Hackney; Shoful
Hansom Patent Safety Cab, 22
Hertz, John, 39–51, 54, 59, 72, 73, 138
Hertz automobile. *See* Ambassador automobile
Hertz Corporation, 44–49
Hicksville, N.Y., 112, 118
Highway Act of 1973 (sect. 16 of UMT Act), 96
Hobson, Tobias, 11
Hogan, Thomas B., 57
Horse cab, 34
Horsecar, 18–19, 28. *See also* Streetcar
Huntington Park, Pa., 129–31

Illinois, 109–15
Illinois Motor Vehicle Law (1921), 66
Immigration, 24–27. *See also* Urban densities
Independent contractor, 3, 94, 104–5, 161–65; IRS policy concerning, 162–64; NLRB policy concerning, 162–63; absence of right of control, 163
Indianapolis, Ind., 144
Innovations, 5, 123–40; integrated service, 123–40 passim, 158–59; markets, 127; organization, 127; paratransit services, 123; diversification, 138–40, 166–67; shared-ride feeder service, 158, 167. *See also* Taxicab services
Insurance, 54–55, 65–71, 119
Integrated paratransit-transit, 4–6, 124, 127, 133–34, 157–60
Internal combustion engine (Otto), 24

Internal Revenue Service (IRS), 86, 105, 157, 162–64; policy on independent contractor status, 65, 157, 162–64
International Brotherhood of Teamsters, 95
International City Managers Association, 83, 102
International Taxicab Association (ITA), 59, 104, 107, 110, 116–19, 171, 176

Jacobs, Walter, 44–48
Jehu, 13
Jitney, 62–64, 127, 135

Kahn, Alfred E., 147, 151
Kalamazoo, Mich., 50, 56
Kansas City, Mo., 27, 43, 141
Kaufman, Frank, 58
Kaufman, Kenneth, 58
Kelly, Edward J., 81
Kettering, Charles, 31
Kinston, N.C., 138

Labor: unions, 34, 94–96; relations with management, 41–42, 94–96; federal regulations, 87; issues, 87, 94–100, 103–6, 161–66; costs, 101, 119, 159
La Mesa, Cal., 129–31
Lamoreaux, Paul, 52
Lawrence, Mass., 138
Lazard Freres, 55
Leasing: status of lessee, 3, 95, 104–5, 161–65; of hackney cabs, 10, 11, 54; public liability of lessor, 16, 17; of taxicabs, 68, 95, 103–6, 127, 139, 165; percentage of taxicabs leased, 105. *See also* Independent contractor
Lenior, Etienne, 32
Levine, Nat, 58
Licenses for drivers, 16–17, 66–68, 80–82, 142; fees for, 15
Licenses for hackney cabs and coaches, 14–15; limitation of numbers of, 15–19
Licenses for taxicabs: limitation of numbers of, 65–72, 80–83, 92, 142–54; passenger vehicles without, 82. *See also* New York City, medallions
Little Rock, Ark., 129, 132
Live clock, 113
Livery, 10, 54
Locomotives on the Highways Act, 28
Lomberg, 49
London, 8–21, 26–27, 34–35
London General Omnibus Company, 18
London Hackney Carriage Act (1831), 16
London Hackney Carriages Act (1843), 16
Los Angeles, Cal., 80, 93, 129–30

McCulloch, Charles A., 51
Management: and organizational structure, 107–8, 164–66; and actions of, 164–69; diversification, 166–67; and public image 167–69
Markin, Morris, 39, 49–53, 56–60
Massachusetts, 70
Mass transit: history, 4–6, 10, 17–19; integrated service, 4–6, 60, 123, 157; public ownership of, 5, 88–89, 158; power of vehicles, 28–30, 62; fares, 62; transition during Depression, 63–65; ridership of, 64, 74–75, 84–85; market, 64–65, 73–75, 84–91; subsidy of, 86–91, 101–2, 128–38, 154–58; government subsidy for competition with taxicabs, 90–91, 96–100, 172; deficits, 123, 158. *See also* Bus; Horsecar; Jitneys; Omnibus; Streetcar
Masters, Claude, 58
Maunoury, Michel Joseph, 37
Medallions. *See* New York City, entry restrictions, medallions
Meter. *See* Taximeter
Miami, Fla., 141
Michigan, 128, 134
Miller, Ernest, 52
Minibus, 23
Mini fleets, 92

Minimum wage, 152
"Miracle of the Marne," 37
Monrovia, Cal., 130–31
Montgomery, Ala., 29, 138
Moore, Henry Charles, 12, 20–24, 34
Morris, Henry, 31
Morrison, William, 31
Motor Carrier Act of 1935, 61, 149
Motor Vehicle Law of Illinois, 66
Muntz, Earl, 90
Muntz Cab Company, 80
Murita, Charles, 58

National Association of Taxicab Owners (NATO), 54, 59, 70, 83
National Labor Relations Act, 87
National Labor Relations Board (NLRB), 87, 157, 162–63; policy on independent contractors, 157
National Mass Transportation Assistance Act, 90
National Transportation Company, 50, 58
Natural monopoly, 147–51
New Haven, Conn., 99
New Mexico, 107
New York City, 6, 18, 26–27, 30; taxicabs in, 6, 18, 26–30, 35, 38, 43, 48–51, 56, 66–67, 70–71, 75–79, 82, 92–96, 118, 125, 143, 146; medallions in, 6, 51, 66–67, 70–71, 82, 92–93, 143, 146; omnibus in, 18; taxicab fares in, 18, 67, 146; growth of, 26, 27, 67; density of, 27–29; steam railways in, 28; cable cars in, 29; electric cabs in, 32–36; taxicab fleets in, 43; entry restrictions in, 66–67, 70–71, 143, 146; unemployment of drivers in, 67; fleets in, during World War II, 75, 78; decline of fleets in, 92–94; mini fleets in, 92; unions in, 95–6
New York Taxicab Association, 35
North Carolina, 107–12, 115, 118, 142
Northeastern Illinois Planning Commission (NIPC): taxicab passengers, 110–11; taxicab trips, 113; dial-a-bus costs, 119; use of taxicab meters, 116

Oakland, Ralph E., 49, 52, 57
Oak Ridge, Tenn., 137
Office of Defense Transportation, (ODT) 77–78, 86
Ohio, 107
Olds, Ransome, 32
Omnes, M., 17
Omnibus, 17–19, 28–29, 35, 64, 65; fares of, 18; steam powered, 29. *See also* Streetcar; Tram
Omnibus Corporation, 48–49
Ontario, Cal., 130–31
Open entry (free entry), 65–67, 70–71, 82, 104, 142–51, 155; Indianapolis experiment, 144–45. *See also* Deregulation; Entry controls; Taxicab industry, limitation of numbers of licenses
Operators, 5, 6, 52, 91, 94, 103–6, 165, 173–75; and private ownership, 5, 173–75; single-taxi firms (owner-operators), 6, 103. *See also* Taxicab operations
Orange County, Cal., 134
Organization, taxicab industry. *See* Taxicab; Taxicab Industry
Otto, Nicholas August, 32
Otto 4-cycle engine, 24
Owner-driver (owner-operator), 52, 91, 94, 103–6, 141, 165. *See also* Drivers

Packard, James, 32
Packard automobile, 104
Packard cab, 76, 85
Pacoina, Cal., 130–31
Paramount Cab Company, 50
Paratransit, 4, 5, 19, 23–24, 33, 123–40 passim, 158. *See also* Integrated paratransit-transit
Paratransit policy statement. *See* Urban Mass Transportation Administration, paratransit policy of

Paratransit vehicle, 176–77
Paris, 9–11, 17–19, 26–27, 33, 37
Parmelee, Frank, 51
Parmelee Transportation Company, 48–51, 82
Pascal, Blaise, 17
Pennsylvania, 109–12
People's Cab Company, 82
Peoples Motor Bus Company, 43
Pepys's *Diary*, 10, 20, 181 (n. 8)
Peterborough, Ont., 134
Pettit, John, 53–54
Philadelphia, Pa., 27–29, 33, 43, 82, 165
Philadelphia Rapid Transit Company, 93
Philadelphia Yellow Cab Company, 93
Pittsburgh, Pa., 53, 75, 82, 99, 114
Place de fiacre, 11
Plying for hire (cruising), 11
Pneumatic tires, 34
Portland, Ore., 141, 144
Presidents' Conference Committee (PCC) streetcar, 64
Private ownership (taxicabs), 5
Provider subsidy. *See* Taxicabs
Public convenience and necessity, certificates of, 70
Public involvement in transit, 101–2
Public ownership (mass transit), 5
Public programs, 6, 7, 173–75; and private operators, 173–75
Public transportation: in ancient times, 8; in Middle Ages, 8, 9; post-World War II, 84, 85
Public Utilities Holding Company Act of 1935, 65

Quadricycle, 32

R & V Motors Company, 43
Rae, J. F., 31–32
Rascob, J. J., 183 (chap. 4, n. 4)
Red Cab Company, 55
Red Flag Law, 29
Reformation, 9

Regulation, 14–17, 65–72, 78–82, 105, 141–155; and hackney, 14, 19; maximum number, 19, 65, 71, 78–81, 141, 147; by states, 65–66, 70–73, 142, 147; and hackney cabs (carriages), 14, 15; and jitneys, 64; insurance, 65–66, 70, 71; entry controls, 65–67, 70–71, 78–81, 141, 144, 147; of fares, 65–66, 70–71, 141–43; public demand for, 65, 69–72, 141; of vehicle condition, 72; by municipalities, 105, 144; ambiguities of, 143–44; minimum number, 144; of shared-ride, 160–61. *See also* Taxicab; Federal Communications Commission; Internal Revenue Service; National Labor Relations Board; Office of Defense Transportation
Rehabilitation Act of 1973, 135–36
Renaissance, 9
Renault taxicab, 54
Richard I, 14
Richmond, Va., 29
Ritchie, John A., 43
Robie, Richard S., 55
Roger-Benz taxicab, 33
Rothschild, W. Lansing, 39, 53–54, 58, 72, 93
Ruinous competition and natural monopoly, 148–52

St. Louis, Mo., 27
Salom, Pedro, 31
Samuels, Benjamin, 57, 58
Samuels, Robert E., 58
San Bernardino, Cal., 130–31
San Diego, Cal., 141–45, 165
San Francisco, Cal., 29, 53–54, 82, 93, 165
San Francisco Veterans Cabs, 82
San Francisco Yellow Cab Company, 53–54, 93
Saunders, Sir Duncomb, 11
Saunders System, Inc., 44
Sawyer, Frank, 39, 52–55, 70
Schoful. *See* Shoful

Seafarers International Union, 95
Seattle, Wash., 104, 141–45, 152
Sedan chairs, 11, 12
Service. *See* Taxicab services
Service innovations. *See* Taxicab services
Shared-ride, 5, 73, 101, 124–32, 142, 158–61, 167. *See also* Taxicab services
Shaw, Walden W., 40–41
Sherman Antitrust Act, 82–83, 87
Shillibeer, George, 18
Shillibeer, 18
Shoful, 22, 182 (nn. 27, 28)
Shopping, 151–52
Showfull. *See* Shoful
Sign of St. Fiacre Inn, 11
Simpson, Hawley, 71, 87
Sinnott, Carol J., 58
Sinnott, James P., 58
Skimming (cream skimming), 151–52
Smerk, G. M., 30
Smith, A. O., 51, 54
Smith, C. Arnholt, 93
Sokoll, Michael, 52
Specialized service. *See* Taxicab services
Sprague, Frank, 29, 64
Stand (standing), 10, 11, 16, 20, 42, 55; standing for hire, 16; private, 42, 55
Stanley, Francis, 31
Stanley, Freelan, 31
Stanley Steamer automobile, 31
Steam engine (automobile), 24, 31
Steam transit, 28–29
Stephenson, John, 28
Stoppelmann, Ronald, 58
Streetcar, 18–19, 25, 28–30, 62–65; horsecars, 18–19, 28; fares, 62; market, 64–65, 84; PCC car, 64–65
Styx River, 8
Subscription bus. *See* Paratransit
Subscription service, 5, 123. *See also* Taxicab services
Subsidy, 6, 87–102 passim, 128–38, 156–58; government competition by, 94; providers, 136; user-side, 136–38
Supply characteristics. *See* Economics of taxicab operations; Taxicab operations
Surface Transportation Act of 1978, 91

Taxicab: ancestors of, 8–24; transportation before, 19, 27, 32–85 passim; vehicles, 33–38, 46, 48, 68, 75–78, 176–77; paratransit services, 33, 123, 138–40; electric-powered vehicles, 33–36; vehicles from Darracq, 35; word, origin of, 35; Paris, 37; manufacture of, 42–44, 48–51, 74–83; manufacture of, by Yellow Cab Manufacturing Company, 42–44, 48; vehicles from Yellow Cab Manufacturing Company, 42–44, 48; manufacture of, by Checker Motors Corporation, 48–52; manufacture of, by De Soto, 50; vehicles from Checker Motors Corporation, 75–76, 85; vehicles from Packard, 76, 85. *See also* Taxicab services
Taxicab industry, 3–7, 25, 33, 38–60, 65–75, 81, 86–108, 138–69, 172–80; image of, 3–7, 41–42, 53, 73, 102, 167–69; private ownership of, 5, 173–75; public funding of, 5, 6; limitation of numbers of licenses, 15–29, 70–72, 80–83, 92, 142–55; fleets, 38–60, 91–96, 107; in World War I, 38; evaluation of, 40–60, 65; franchises, 43, 81; Depression in, 65–73; regulation of, 65, 70–71, 141–55; in World War II, 75; and Federal Communications Commission, 86; transit subsidies as competition for, 87–91, 101–2, 128–38, 156–58; federal funds for taxis, 96–100; transit policy as competition for, 96; organization and structure of, 103–8; management actions and future of, 107–8, 164–69, 175–80; economic trends and the future, 122; survival of, 139–40, 172; and imper-

fections, 151–54. See also Depression; Entry controls; Management; Regulation; Taxicab operations

Taxicab operations, 5–7, 33–38, 41–43, 53–58, 60, 65–73, 76, 79, 83, 87, 94–100, 103–10, 113–22, 127, 129–33, 136–55, 161–66, 176–77; and public funding, 6; shortages of fuel, 7, 57, 86; stands, 10–11, 42, 45; cruising, 11; vehicles, 33–38, 45–48, 69–70, 176–77; tires, 34, 43–44, 104; maintenance, 41, 53, 76, 93, 164, 166; deadheading, 42; management, 41–44, 164–66; war and postwar ridership, 46–52, 84–85; insurance, 54–55, 65–71, 119; computers, use of, 57–58; war and postwar, 75–85; fringe benefits for drivers, 94, 103, 165; fuel, 104; costs, 116–19, 138; revenues, 117–18; economic trends, 122; taxi-transit integration, 157–60; diversification, 166–67. See also Dispatching; Drivers; Economics of taxicab operations; Fares; Independent contractor; Labor; Leasing; Operators; Regulation

Taxicab services, 3–6, 62–66, 73, 78–79, 84–85, 96–97, 101–2, 110–13, 123–40, 151–53, 157–61, 166–69, 173–77; package, mail, and message delivery, 3, 126–27, 167; paratransit, 4, 19, 24, 123–40 passim; shared-ride, 4, 5, 73, 96–101, 124–32, 142, 158–61, 167; neighborhood circulation, 5, 134; street hail for, 5, 127, 151; subscription, 5, 123, 127; jitney, 62–64, 127, 135; market for, 66, 84–85, 128–38, 151; minibus, 125; school bus, 125–27; taxi pools for, 127, 135; charter (plan-a-ride) of, 127, 132; market for general market services, 128–35; market requiring subsidies, 128–29; options for, 132; plan-a-ride, 132–33; market for target market services, 135–38; brokerage of, 137, 159; transit failures, filling gap left by, 159–60. See also Demand characteristics; Elderly and handicapped persons; Integrated paratransit-transit

Taximeter, 3, 13, 35, 70, 73
Taylor, G. R., 18
Teamsters. See International Brotherhood of Teamsters
Terminal Taxicab Company, 48
Tidewater Transportation District, 134
Town Cab Company, 55
Toye, Frank, 58
Toye, George, 58
Toye, George, Jr., 58
Traffic lights, 42, 45, 138
Tram, 18. See also Streetcar
Transport Workers Union (TWU), 95

Unions, 35, 94–95
United States: growth of, 25–26; immigration into, 25–26
United States government, 25, 82–91, 96–101, 109–15, 137, 139, 157, 162–63, 171. See also various government departments and agencies listed alphabetically
Ur, 9
Urban densities, 9, 26–27, 30
Urban growth, 25–27, 30, 38
Urban Mass Transportation Act (UMT Act), 90, 98–101, 134; section 3e of, 90, 98, 100; section 5 of, 90; section 12c-6 of, 98; section 13c of, 98–101, 134; section 16 of, 96–98
Urban Mass Transportation Administration (UMTA), 91, 96–100, 137, 139; funding by, 91, 96–97, 135, 137; paratransit policy of, 96–100; transit policy of, 96–100

Van pool, 123
Veterans cabs, 57, 79–85

Veterans Taxicab Company, 82
Victoria, 23
Vidich, Charles, 66
Visions of the future, 171–73; private enterprise in public transportation, 172; public programs and private operators, 173

Walden W. Shaw Livery Company, 41
Walker, James, 70
War Veterans Taxicab Association, 80
Washington, D.C., 53, 68, 75, 82, 143
Watermen (of hackney horses), 12
Weber, A. F., 26, 30
Weiss, Henry, 50
Wells, John D., 105–6, 117–21, 125, 139
Westgate Corporation, 54, 58, 93
Wherry, 8, 10, 181 (n. 1)
William IV, 23
Wilson, Woodrow, 63
Windshields, 44, 46
Windshield wipers, 44
Winton, Alexander, 32
Wisconsin, 107, 109
World War I, 37–38, 62
World War II, 50, 57, 60, 63–64, 74–85, 141, 160

Yellow, 42
Yellow Cab companies, 43
Yellow Cab Company (Chicago), 42, 48, 52, 56–57, 66, 69, 78, 81–82
Yellow Cab Company (Los Angeles), 53–54, 80
Yellow Cab Company (New Orleans), 58
Yellow Cab Company (San Francisco), 53–54
Yellow Cab Company of California, 54
Yellow Cab Company of Phoenix, 54
Yellow Cab Company of Pittsburgh, 56, 58
Yellow Cab Company of Stroudsburg, Pa., 132
Yellow Cab Manufacturing Company, 42–43, 47–48, 54
Yellow cabs, 3, 66, 80
Yellow Drive-It-Yourself Company, 44
Yellow Taxi Company of Minneapolis, 56, 58

Zone rates, 116–17
Zoning, 38

www.ingramcontent.com/pod-product-compliance
Lightning Source LLC
Chambersburg PA
CBHW021405290426
44108CB00010B/388